# Memoirs of a Ginger Cat

# Memoirs of a Ginger Cat

Curt Scarborough

Tampa, Florida

The content associated with this book is the sole work and responsibility of the author. Gatekeeper Press had no involvement in the generation of this content.

Memoirs of a Ginger Cat

Published by Gatekeeper Press
7853 Gunn Hwy., Suite 209
Tampa, FL 33626
www.GatekeeperPress.com

Copyright © 2024 by Curt Scarborough
All rights reserved. Neither this book nor any parts within it may be sold or reproduced in any form or by any electronic or mechanical means, including information storage and retrieval systems, without permission in writing from the author. The only exception is by a reviewer, who may quote short excerpts in a review.

The cover design, interior formatting, typesetting, and editorial work for this book are entirely the product of the author. Gatekeeper Press did not participate in and is not responsible for any aspect of these elements.

Library of Congress Control Number: TBD

ISBN (paperback): 9781662959547

# Dedication

To
beloved companions
we expect to see
again someday

Seara
Summer
Gidget (Alice)
Angel (Elizabeth)
Lady Long Legs
Dottie Moon
Quirky Rex

plus, a multitude of
other 4-legged friends
too numerous to mention

# Table of Contents

# Foreword from Leo

Since this is my first swipe at being a writer, I need to make a couple of things straight right off the bat.

First, although these are strictly true tales about my nine lives, Daddy Curt is doing the typing, and he may not be totally trustworthy. He has been known to stretch the truth far beyond the believability point. In fact, he admitted this flaw in his otherwise sterling silver character in the title of a book he wrote a couple of years ago: "I Can Remember Anything (*whether it happened or not*)."

Secondly, Momma Roni is doing the proofreading, which causes me to purr with great trepidation, whatever that is. Here's the thing. She has a severe allergy to corny jokes, and she usually censors Dad's materials before they go to the publisher. Yet sometimes a groaner of a story slips by her joke-filter, and if you run across one of those, just remember this. Dad is not only a stretcher, but he is also a cornball, and Mom may have missed a clinker in her eagerness to keep everything clean around this house . . . especially his stories.

So, with those precautionary warnings, polish your spectacles and read on.

- Leonardo De Cattio

# 1

# Hello, North Dakota!

On July 21, 2010, my mother, Flossie De Cattio, gave birth to sextuplets; I was #6. She was a petite ginger cat with long orange-blonde hair, who labored hard to corral her brood. I never saw my cat father, whom Momma called Alphonso Slick. I imagine him as a traveling salesman, who peddled his wares on the backroads of the Dakotas in the early 21st Century. I see him as offering rock bottom deals on washboards, lightning rods, and whatnot. I think maybe Momma ended up getting one of his bargain whatnots.

Ours was a single-parent family consisting of Momma, two males and four females of the opposite sex. The trio of tortoise shell female girls were named Patricia, Laverne, and Maxine. Momma was crazy about the Andrews Sisters on the radio.

My other sister was named Donna, but she was so stuck-up, we all called her Prima. When humans came to the farm to see the new arrivals, they invariably picked up that showy calico, Donna. They'd hold her and say, "You are the most beautiful girl I've ever seen." And she would put on a fake smile like a Cheshire and with a supercilious meow reply, "I know!" Frankly, it was sickening, because anyone with two eyes and a modicum of good taste could plainly see that I was much better looking . . . plus, I was softer and fuzzier too.

My brother was an all-white fellow, who sported a short haircut. He was named after our roaming dad, but we called him Alf for short. I was the sixth kit to pop onto the scene . . . and, they say, I was the runt of the litter. However, I always remind naysayers, "I may be last but I'm not the least! Remember that dynamite comes in small packages!" (I always get a big bang out of that one . . . hopefully, Mom Roni won't censor out that sparkling gem as too corny.)

*Parenthetically, have you noticed my rather extensive vocabulary? This is an outgrowth of my curiosity and inquisitive personality. You see, every time I hear an unfamiliar word, I make up a definition for it and use in it a sentence three times that same day. Yes indeed . . . I am extensively inquisitively parenthetic!*

My mother, Flossie, told me that, although I was the only one of her children who looked like her, when she first laid her eyes on me, she thought she had given birth to a ferocious lion. Of course, my pathetic "meow" instead of a thundering roar soon dissipated that erroneous notion. She said that at first, she wanted to name me Bert Laur, but she figured nobody would get the Wizard of Oz reference. So instead, she named me Leonardo Dr. Cattio, (Leo for short).

The first couple of weeks after my initial birthday, I noticed very little about my surroundings. Then one fine sunny morning in early August, my eyes opened, and "HELLO, NORTH DAKOTA!"

What I saw caused me to shut my eyes tight again and call for my Momma. There, looking me right in the eye, was a huge ghostly-pale monster with doggy-breath, licking my face. I figured the creature was salivating me all over so that I could slide down his throat quickly in one gulp! As it turns out, it wasn't actually a scary, hairy monster at all, although that pooch indeed was a pretty formidable carnivore. She was the family's friendly yellow Labrador, Sierra, who appointed herself as my official guide to life on the farm.

We resided on a few acres just outside the village of Edgeley, located in the southeastern corner of North Dakota. Edgeley had a papulation of 585 people, plus a whole passel of livestock which usually were not counted (unless they were Republicans) in the official census to determine the number of representatives we deported to Washington, D.C.

Seirra gave me the twenty-five-cent tour around the farm which I prefer to call a cattle ranch because that sounds more exotic and western cowboyish. My human family, Charlie and Roni Mastel, owned a herd of Angus cattle, which roamed the pasture for a mile or so in each direction, I guess. I always remained pretty close to the house, and my cat family usually stayed in the yard, sleeping in the barn unless it was a clear and warmish night when they camped out under the stars. I preferred to stay cuddled up inside with my mom and brother and sisters when it got a little chilly. North Dakota winters have a reputation for chilliness.

One day my mom and siblings started scurrying around in the yard, and excitedly headed out to the barn because, they said, a rainstorm was coming. As the brave lion of the bunch, I didn't flee for shelter . . . until it was almost too late to vamoose. I got caught in a huge gulley-washer of a typhoon and barely made it under the porch to keep from getting swept away into the pond. I huddled there meowing as loud as I could for help.

Finally, Daddy Charlie heard me and told his wife, Momma Roni. She came out into the downpour and coaxed me into her loving arms. She took a photo of me, and I candidly admit that snapshot would not win a beauty contest, unless the judges had a preferential bias toward drowned rats. She carried me into the house, dried me off, and fed me a yummy meal. Then she allowed me to snuggle down with her on the bed . . . and the rest, as they say, is motion picture history.

Instantly, I was transformed from an outdoor cat into an indoor cat. In fact, I never ventured outside the house after that fateful encounter with doom. Why should I? I had it made, and my life henceforth was just like a delightful ball of yarn.

At least for a while.

# 2

# Everybody's Got to Be Somewhere

North Dakotans are not wishy-washy. There in the Roughrider State, it's either black or white. There's no such thing as a gray area. Here's what I mean by that.

We refuse to waste money paying for an air-conditioner in our pickups, although an industrial-sized heater is worth a fortune to us. If our truck has a radio, it must be pre-turned to the Lawrence Welk Polka station (a1-a2), with farm news and mooo-ed music 24 hours a day.

It's either summertime or wintertime in ND. One day it's 70 degrees Fair-in-height; the next day it's 70 below zero. The only fall around here is what the temperature does following the four weeks of summer that we enjoy between Flag Day and the 4th of July . . . then overnight, it's winter!

And here-abouts, a joke is either a knee-slapper or you're too dense to appreciate sophisticated Swedish humor. Like, for example, this favorite story of Daddy Charlie:

*A farmer is toting bags of feed across the backyard to the pigpen about a hundred yards away. His friend says, "Why don't you park your pick-up right up close to the pen? It would save a lot of time." The farmer replies, "What's time to a pig?"*

My human Daddy, Charlie Mastel, was a great example of the typical hard-working blue-collar guy of the Midwest. He had a macho-tough exterior, but inside, he was a marshmallow. He never allowed himself to take a day off from the farm/ranch chores, assisted by his wife Roni, (a shortened version of her given name, Veronica.) He also had other occupations . . . selling and erecting fences and decks, representing a cable TV company, selling real estate, and being the community go-to guy when a neighbor needed any handyman tasks done. All this, in spite of a very serious heart problem and various other terminal ailments. Tough Germans in North Dakota have a rigorous work ethic . . . and Daddy Charlie was work-ethical to the nth degree.

Both Momma Roni and I warned him about his overworking, and we were very worried about his health, but he pushed on relentlessly, day after day. When he dragged himself in at night, he was totally exhausted. After supper, he always just slouched and dozed off in a stuffed chair in the living room with Gidget on his lap.

Oh, that's right. I haven't told you yet about Gidget, the black tiger cat, who was strictly a "Charlie's girl." She was the indoor-outdoor feline of the household. She and I, along with a calico named Angel, were the only cats allowed into the Mastel ranch house. About 50 or 100 other cats camped outside the back door at suppertime, but I'll talk more about them later on.

Gidget was a wise, elderly girl who had been born on the ranch about 2003, so she was at least 7 cat-years old when I met her. (I don't know how many that is in human-years.) She had been everywhere in the four neighboring states, hunting and fishing, and she knew the answer to any and all questions that Angel and I asked her. Gidget . . . it's a goofy name, which, Angel said, was short for "Girl-Midget." Angel was clever enough, however, not to mention that slanderous term in front of the black tiger cat.

It was between Halloween and Christmas of 2010, and I had settled into the household routine, when Sierra became terminally ill . . . so bad that she could barely walk and wouldn't eat.

*I pause here to correct an error we made in chapter one. According to Momma Roni, my friend the yellow Lab was named SEARA, not SIERRRA as originally reported. Daddy Curt, who is typing this manuscript, stubbornly insists on using the spelling from the Humphrey Bogart classic, "The Treasure of Sierra Madre," but that's his problem. I'm going along with Momma; she ought to know, since she named that canine herself.*

Seara howled and moaned ceaselessly for several days, and everyone knew that she was getting too weak to make it much longer. One morning Daddy Charlie took her out for a walk away off beyond the cattle pond. An hour later he returned home alone and told Momma, "Seara won't be coming home anymore." Momma cried, and kind of surprisingly, so did Daddy Charlie. Angel and I felt sorry too, although we didn't quite understand what had happened.

Two or three weeks later, on December 17th . . . just a few days before Christmas . . . Gidget came into the room where I was sleeping very early in the morning. She told me to follow her into the living room. There lying on the floor was Daddy Charlie, and he was cold, and he wasn't moving. She told me to go gently wake up Momma Roni and bring her into the front room. Gidget laid down between Daddy Charlie's outstretched legs to stand guard.

When Momma Roni saw Daddy Charlie lying on the floor, she immediately called a neighbor who was a highway policeman. He came to help, but it was too late, he said. Soon some other men came and took Daddy Charlie away. Momma held me tight in her arms and said, "Daddy Charlie won't be coming home anymore." Then lots of other folks came by to visit Momma. Everybody seemed sad and talked very softly about what a good man Daddy Charlie had been, and how much they were going to miss him.

Friends and neighbors came and went regularly for several days. And that helped Momma to get her mind off the hurt that she felt from being alone now, except for Gidget, Angel, and me. The two feline girls took a vote and appointed me as the official Comfort Cat, since, although I was the last one to show up in the household, I was the closest to Momma, because I slept in her bed.

So, every night after all the visitors had come and gone, and Momma Roni had locked the doors, she sat in the sunroom on her favorite chair and held me on her lap. We talked about missing Seara and Daddy Charlie. She reminded me that one of his favorite sayings was, "Everybody's got to be somewhere." That is true, I suppose, and it helped a little bit, but not a whole lot. Sure, my best friend, Seara, and her husband, Charlie, were somewhere. The problem was . . . they weren't here.

# 3 Ramblings by the Ramrod of the Ranch

The Mastel Cattle Ranch was owned by Charlie and Roni, so they were the big bosses of the outfit, of course. They boasted a crew of several ranch hands around the place, if you count all the cats and other livestock. They were in the calving business, and so they owned cows and a bull and a barn and everything.

Against Charlie's advice, Roni had a bad habit of naming the calves when they were born. She invariably got emotionally involved. Truthfully, she bawled like a calf in a hailstorm whenever one of her babies got shipped off to the market. "Buddy" was her first calf, and since he arrived in the wintertime, Roni brought him inside the house and let him sleep on the old couch in the basement, where one of the dogs usually slept. She pampered another young bull (Spenser) who cornered her in the corral one day, and almost cracked four of her ribs. They sent him on his way to the auction pronto.

But Roni's favorite bigger-than-a-cat animals were donkeys. She had five of them, which she named Sebastian, Jasmin, Levi, Sammy, and Sheba. She was quick to defend the reputation of those stubborn animals, claiming that they were sweet, loving, misunderstood . . . and deserving of our sincerest respect and fondest admiration. She immediately pounced on and censored my clever little quip that the reason folks don't send donkeys to college is because, "Nobody likes a smart ass!"

"Yep," as Gary Cooper said, The Mastels had quite a spread there in the Dakota Territory. But the number one, top-hand, main Ramrod on the ranch was a tough-talking, hard-drinking, fast- shooting sidewinder named Gidget. At least that's what she claimed whenever she got high on catnip and took a notion to reminisce.

One wintry night, for example, Ramrod Gidget invited Angel and me to join her behind the furnace in the basement where she kept her private stash of 90-proof catnip. There she regaled us with one tall tale after another, which she swore on a stack of hot tamales were the truth, the whole truth, and nothing like the truth. Frankly, I wondered about a few of her questionable details, but I never mentioned those doubts to Calamity Gidget. Otherwise, I probably wouldn't be here today to write this book.

Here is Gidget's tale, in her own words:

> "I was in a roadhouse in the Badlands one night in '09, when a 3-legged dog limped into the saloon and said to the bartender, "I'm lookin' for the guy who shot my paw." (Leo's note: I didn't know whether this was a lame joke or not, so I just grinned a little and purred louder . . . Gidget continues.) Which reminds me, have either of you young whippersnappers noticed that I limp a little bit on my port-side? Let me tell you about getting the war wound that crippled me up a bit.
>
> *"I was out doing a little bird hunting in the bar ditch alongside the hard road, when a half-drunk moose driving a weed-whacker machine swerved intentionally to try to run me over.*

*I leaped out of the way, but he clipped me on my right haunch, and I was left dazed and wounded on the side of the road. I was starting to bleed-out, but I dragged myself up to the ranch house. Momma Roni was outside in her garden, and she heard me coming. As a former nurse, she immediately sprang into action and administered first aid and second aid to bandage me up. I spent a couple of days in ICU . . . all the time plotting revenge against that killer moose named Roscoe.*

*"I discovered through my extensive research that a moose has only one weakness. They are crazy about peas. Other veggies are good, they say, but nothing is more satisfying than a good pea. And, oddly, the felonious moose sub-species I was after savors each individual pea separately, eating them slowly one by one.*

*"So, my diabolical plan was formed, and if I do say so myself . . . (and I do say so myself) . . . this was fiendishly clever. I dug a 13-foot-deep hole and filled it halfway to the top with ashes. I sprinkled frozen peas all around the rim of the hole. Then I hid in the bushes and waited for my prey to arrive and take the bait.*

*"Pretty soon Roscoe, the killer moose, came along. When he bent over to take a pea, I kicked him in the ash-hole."*

So that was the end of the Roscoe story, as Gidget dozed off and began snoring softly. This tall tale explains Gidget's dubious claim to have eaten not only a goose, but also a moose. Maybe she did; I'm not sure. I personally observed her once devouring a whole chicken, beak, feet, feathers and all. And another time, on Momma Roni's birthday, Gidget presented her with a very deceased gopher carcass.

Momma, ever the perfect hostess, thanked her politely and called the undertaker, Daddy Charlie, to take care of the burial details. However, before the funeral service, mysteriously the corpse disappeared . . . and Gidget was heard letting out a tiny little burp.

A few years later, when Gidget was about seven, Momma Roni and family (Gidget, Angel, and yours truly) moved to Missouri. There we got a new dad, when Momma Rone married Daddy Curt. He welcomed us and christened the girls with new names. Gidget became Alice N. Wanderland, because she wandered a lot and reminded him of the Cheshire cat of storybook fame. Angel was renamed Elizabeth Tailer (spelling is correct) because of her purple eyes, feisty personality, and shapely torso which reminded him of the movie star by the almost-same name. He just kept on calling me Leo . . . although, I think, it may have been Daddy Curt who originally came up with my classy moniker, Leonardo De Cattio.

# 4

# How Cold Is It?

My best subject in school was Geography. Believe it or not, I went through Edgeley, ND high school in less than twenty minutes. I could have gone through a whole lot faster, but I got stuck at the cafeteria. They were serving "mystery-meat" . . . my favorite. One of the things I learned in school that day was that there are an estimated 40 or more states in the US of A, and they're all quite different.

A 10-o'clock scholar easily can tell you what each state is notorious for, or what it is famous because of. (I double-dog-dare you to diagram that sentence!) For instance, if I say "Idaho," you'll immediately think of mashed potatoes, right? Or French fries. And if I mention "California," you'll think of movie stars and swimming pools, or movie stars in swimming pools. "Nevada" brings to mind crap-shooting; "Illinois" is Lincoln-land; and when "The eyes of Texas are upon you" . . . you'll Remember the Alamo.

Furthermore, "Wisconsin" evokes Pabst Blue Ribbon and cheese-heads; "Iowa" is definitely corny; "Arizona depicts cactuses . . . or is it cacti's? (No matter!) And "New Jersey" conjures up, who else? . . . Spiro Agnew. I could go on . . . but you get the point here, I'm sure.

Which brings us to my home state of North Dakota. Tell me the truth. When I mentioned this state, didn't you immediately think of snow, and blizzards, and temperatures colder than kraut?

There are over fifty thousand jokes about North Dakota's weather, and I really mean it, and I'm not kidding one tiny little bit. 'Cause Momma warned me a million times not to exaggerate.

So, after an extensive survey from my yuck-yuck man-on-the-street pollster, here are the ten best North Dakota knee-slappers, in answer to this leading weather question: "How cold is it?"

It was so cold that . . .

10. I saw a bus drive by, and the greyhound was inside.
9. Chickens were rushing into KFC to use the deep fryer.
8. Prisoners were begging to be sent to the electric chair.
7. I saw an Amish man buy an electric blanket.
6. I chipped my tooth on my soup.
5. I had to open my fridge to heat the house.
4. My teeth were chattering and they're still in the glass.
3. Starbucks started serving mocha on a stick.
2. I saw a politician putting his hands into his own pockets.
1. People were wearing two pairs of pajamas . . . to Wal-Mart.

So, to pass the long, lonesome winter days and the dark, dreary polar nights, folks in North Dakota do a lot of dropping-in for a neighborly visit and to share some juicy gossipy tid-bits. I don't have time here to list all of Momma Roni's friends, so I'll mention only a few of her closest buds who stopped by most frequently to eat, drink, and be merry.

Probably Momma's closest "Everyday Friend" was a schoolteacher named La Rae. Daddy Curt, who is a whiz with nicknames, started calling her Lash LaRue, and she didn't seem to mind too much. I think she must have been a B-grade cowboy movie aficionado . . . but I'm getting way ahead of my story. Sorry about that.

La Rae dropped over every single day from her house next door . . . which in cow country isn't as close as it sounds. She lived on a farm with her husband, Myron, about two miles away, as the crow flies. (If the crow had to walk, it'd be a little farther.)

As I mentioned, La Rae taught school - fourth grade at Edgeley Elementary, so on weekdays, she dropped by Momma Roni's place around three o'clock to catch each other up on the daily happenings. Usually, I spent those lazy afternoons in what little shade you could find in the sunroom while Momma sat on her queenly throne. La Rae sat across the table, and they talked a lot about this and that and the other thing, which must have dried out their vocal cords because they sipped down quite a large quantity of adult liquid refreshment at happy hour.

Momma favored a half glass of milk, filled to the brim with Scotch, and La Rae was partial to brandy. Peaches, I think, or some other kind of healthy fruit. Only occasionally did I sneak a lick of Momma's libation, but I prefer tea. As a Free Methodist, I am a tea-totaler, but Momma was a strict Lutheran, which was mandated if you were of German extraction and resided in North Dakota. Momma Roni's mother (Constance Burckhardt) was a German immigrant from Russia, and her father (the town dentist, Dr. Ralph Nielson) was Danish. So there you have it.

Momma Roni's other best friends were a young couple, Joe and Katrina (Kat for short.) Joe worked at the Ford dealership, selling cars and mechanic-ing. Kat had purchased a house through Daddy Charlie when he sold real estate, and she got acquainted with Momma because Kat always had to come over to the house to use the telephone. As fate would have it, with an assist from the town's matchmaker (Momma Roni), wedding bells rang for Joe and Kat, and they finally tied the knot after several months of indecisive shuffling around.

About once or twice a week, when Joe got finished at the shop and Kat got home from her job at the animal clinic in Jamestown, the couple would show up at Momma's place for supper. It was an even trade-off. Kat took care of getting all the cats on the farm their shots and check-ups, and Joe kept the tractors and other farm equipment up and running like a top. Truthfully, they became like Momma's beloved son and daughter . . . especially close and supporting to her and me and the other cats after Daddy Charlie was gone.

So, how cold was it in North Dakota in those days? Since I am strictly an indoor cat who stays very close to the fireplace in the wintertime, and who sleeps under the blanket with Momma Roni . . . I really can't tell you from personal experience. Gidget (or Alice, if you prefer) tells me that it's so cold in ND that hell froze over . . . but you know how much she stretches the truth!

# 5

# Sears, Roebuck and Company

A recent quasi-scientific survey of rural households in North Dakota asked the name of the family's favorite or most-read book. The following results were discovered:

| | |
|---|---|
| The Holy Bible | 5% |
| Baby's Photo Album | 10% |
| The Farmer's Almanac | 15% |
| Sears, Robuck Catalog | 70% |

So, the Wish Book outranked the Good Book by 65 points, which is outside the margin of error by a long shot. A follow-up question perhaps revealed the reason for the huge popularity of the mail-order catalog. It had a whole lot more pictures . . . even more than the baby album!

This seg-ways neatly into a continuation of my history of the Leonardo saga. A couple of years passed after Daddy Charlie died, during which Momma Roni sold off all the cattle and donkeys. What a sad day! Then she auctioned off all the farm machinery and other equipment and tools. After that, she had a yard sale to get rid of all the stuff she no longer had any use for . . . taking the highest offer that any shopper made.

She (along with Gidget, Angel, and me) settled down to a quiet existence, visiting friends who dropped in, baby-sitting the children of the highway cop and his wife, attending a Tuesday night Bible study, and worshiping every Sunday morning at the tiny Norton Methodist Church. Lash LaRue dropped by almost every day to inform and imbibe, and Joe and Kat frequently put their feet under Roni's table for a home-cooked meal. Life was peacefully boring . . . and lonesome.

One day, when La Rae was visiting with Momma Roni, I knocked the Sears catalog off the table "accidently", and it fell open to a page advertising men's long johns. I think this nudge of mine must have triggered some weird thoughts because abruptly the ladies started talking about the subject of mail-order brides and mail-order grooms.

Sears, Roebuck and Company of Chicago peddles almost everything you can think of . . . so why not a husband for a lonely widow? Lash and Momma kicked that subject around a while, freshened their drinks a couple of times, and started talking seriously about dating sites on the internet. Momma wasn't very hot on the idea. She said she wouldn't mind having a male pen pal, or maybe even meeting a man someplace safe for a chicken salad sandwich. But, she said, she definitely was not interested in any lovey-dovey stuff.

That night before bedtime, Momma Roni went into her little office and started site surfing . . . is that the right term? Anyhow, she looked up "lonely heart's clubs" and "spouses for sale or rent" and a few others that I never heard of. Finally, after lots of waffling, she picked one and signed up and gave the machine her credit card. Then she started scrolling through the "meat market", as veteran singles-bar patrons like to call the get-with-it activity.

In a few days, after posting her photo and bio, Momma Roni was inundated (that's a punny word "undated", considering she was looking for a date), but I digress. What I mean is that a whole bunch of guys spotted her smiling picture, and immediately pinged to suggest that they would like to get a marriage license . . . or at least a learner's permit. She deleted most of those unsuitable suitors, but she did agree to meet one fellow because he had an animal name and Momma Roni is a sucker for wildlife. I think his first name was Rufus and his last name was some kind of a furry friend . . . maybe Weasel or Ferret.

This fellow, Rufus, was an itinerant handyman from a neighboring town, who also filled-in as a part-time supply preacher at a hard-shell Baptist church. He showed up one afternoon at the farm, and I watched him through the window in the sunroom. He was wearing bib overalls and a straw hat and toting a big black book . . . a King James Bible, I think it was. Momma Roni was sitting on her golf cart, and Rufus walked right up and tried to kiss her on the mouth. But she dodged him and drove off a little way up the lane. He got real mad and preached her one of his fire-and-brimstone sermons. Then he got back into his old beat-up Chevy pickup and roared away back up to the hard road and to his place somewhere in the next county. I was not sorry to see him go, and Momma Roni didn't seem too cut up about it either.

Another fellow who came a-courting was an insurance salesman from way down in Florida whose name was Bill. He was a very old rich millionaire, who originally had come from Georgia, and he flaunted his southern accent which made most of his lady acquaintances swoon with the vapors. Momma Roni and Bill traded emails and talked over the telephone a whole bunch of times, and some of the talk got too mushy for me to repeat here.

They liked each other pretty well, but Gidget, always the sharp-tongued critic who spoke her mind around the ranch, had another opinion about Bill. She said that he was too oily, and "slicker than snot on a doorknob." I think Gidget had been the target of one of Bill's sneaky little kicks under the table, when she wandered too close during suppertime.

Apparently, Bill was a super-salesman with an irresistible spiel, because Momma Roni gave serious consideration to marrying up with that elderly carpetbagger from the Deep South. As I mentioned, Bill had lots of money. But he was a cheapskate and a miser, in my opinion, and Gidget and Angel agreed with my unbiased evaluation. Yet in spite of our not-so-subtle cold-shoulder objections, and some wise cautions from her friends in Edgeley, Momma Roni made up her mind that Bill probably would make a good husband and cat-dad for her cozy little family.

Well, all this is just a preliminary to the next chapter, which is the story of the worst time of my nine lives. Of course, I survived that coming catastrophe, so everything turns out okay. But, to tell you the truth, I am kind of sorry that I "accidentally" pushed that Sears catalog off the table. It sure led to some weird happenings . . . but we all made it through okay, and here we are because, as Daddy Charlie used to say, "everybody's got to be somewhere."

# 6

# My Trip to Dizzy-knee-World

"For fabulous family fun, you should go to Florida," everybody said, "and be sure to visit Mickey Mouse's house." That sounded okay to me, although I really prefer Fancy Feast or Meow Mix rather than raw meat. Gidget, however, will swallow anything that doesn't swallow her first. A vegetarian, she is not, never has been, and never will be!

Speaking of swallowing anything . . . Momma Roni swallowed the shiny lure thrown out by Slick Willie, (as we canny cats of ND called him), and she made elaborate preparations to drive two thousand miles southeast to visit that old, rich insurance salesman and his family down in the swampland known as the Sunshine State. I've got to tell you the truth. Gidget, Angel, and I were less than enthusiastic about this proposed trip.

Farm canines, like our late Lab friends Seara and Summer, just loved to hop into the car and go for a drive with their heads hanging out the windows and their tongues flapping in the breeze. But the feline branch of the Mastel clan . . . not so much. In a moving car, I often wanted to hang my head out the window, but only because

I hate to barf on the seat covers. Neatness counts. If the federal government can goose a cow to jump over the moon, I'd like to know why they can't invent a C-sick pill for nauseating cats?

Momma Roni had purchased a new Hyundai on a previous trip to Florida, and she packed this covered wagon to the roof with everything a family of seventeen would ever need in a lifetime. I've got to retract that last statement. She didn't pack it to the roof . . . She also packed stuff on top of the roof. When we pulled out of Edgeley that fateful morning in December of 2013, we looked kind of like the Joad family in "The Grapes of Wrath" leaving Oklahoma for California after the dust bowl during the Great Depression. Except Momma was a whole bunch better looking than Ma Joad was. Henry Fonda, eat your heart out.

The back seat of the sedan was crammed with two cat crates or kennels or hutches or whatever you call those cramped cages. Gidget, because of her seniority I guess, got a private room, with her own personal litter box. Angel and I had to share a single room, with only one potty-place, so not only was it crowded, it also was a little bit embarrassing for me.

You have heard, I am sure, how pilgrims on a trek to the promised land sing as they travel? I am happy to report that the trio from the back seat of Momma's Sonata sang non-stop every eternal mile of the way. I was the lead soprano whiner, hitting the highest and shrillest notes flawlessly, while Angel sang alto-tenor, and Gidget did the bass doo-wops. Fortunately for Momma, she had hearing aids which she could turn off, and she did.

We got snackers from time to time, which muted our singing temporarily. Momma stopped occasionally to take a rest and fill up the gas tank and her supply of sunflower seeds. I tried a couple of those treats, but no thanks. They're okay, but in my book, seeds are for the birds! (I hope Momma lets that one pass uncensored, because seeds aren't really corny.)

It was snowing when we left North Dakota. Friends and neighbors had thrown a big bon voyage farewell party the night before, and we hit the road very early that mid-December morning. Momma planned to make that trip in three legs, and the first stop was Kansas City, MO. We arrived about dark at a Motel 6 just outside of town. Tom Bodette had left a light on for us.

I was relieved when we first arrived . . . then my heart sank, because "Slick Willie" had flown up from Florida to meet us and drive together with us down to his plantation. (Plantation was the name of the town where he lived.) That first night in Kansas City, he wanted to leave the cats out in the car, but Momma wouldn't hear of it because it was too cold. We got to go inside their motel room, but we had to stay in our hutches instead of up on the bed with Momma.

The next day, the backseat trio sang at the top of our lungs in the hope that our unwanted passenger would go crazy and jump out the window. We caused him to squirm and look around kind of mad, and then he put on his earmuffs. But, no matter how off-key we whined, he didn't take the hint and bail out. So, Momma pressed on southward, and pretty soon we ran out of the snowfall and into the tropical breezes of the State of Mississippi.

That night we stopped in Jackson, and Bill insisted that we up-grade from Motel 6, so we threw out our anchor at Motel 8. Unfortunately, they had a "No Pets" policy, so Momma had to sneak us into the room under a quilt she threw over our cages. Slick Willie warned us to keep quiet or he'd throw us outside into that humidity . . . which sounded like something I didn't want to be thrown out into. So, we kept our meows down until we arrived inside.

The room was a tiny bit nicer than the one in KC. Gidget noticed a chocolate on the pillow and jumped up there and gobbled it down in one bite. I had warned her against the danger of eating chocolate, but she told me not to worry about it because that chocolate was moving and it had six legs. I'm not sure what she meant by that, but I was too worn out from singing to ask.

When we finally got to Bill's house in Florida, we discovered that cats were banned from the house because one of his grown sons who lived there was allergic. That meant we cats had to hunker down day and night on the screened-in back porch and suffer through the extreme heat. It was almost Christmas, and we North Dakota residents were used to blizzards and below zero temperatures . . . not 100-degrees with humidity to match.

When Bill deposited us on the back porch, he got out his hose to wash off the dirt that had accumulated there over the summer. I guess he thought it was funny when he "accidently" sprayed Gidget, Angel and me several times until we were soaked to the bone. Actually, we weren't a whole lot wetter than before, as we had sweated profusely from the blazing sun. But getting squirted by our host wasn't the welcoming gesture we expected or deserved. Momma had observed his mean streak and began having second thoughts about their marriage, I think.

That night, back into our respective cages for safety from the prowling raccoons, alligators, and peacocks, I whispered to Angel that I was feeling very, very homesick. She reminded me that now this was our home. And I said, "I know. And I'm sick of it!"

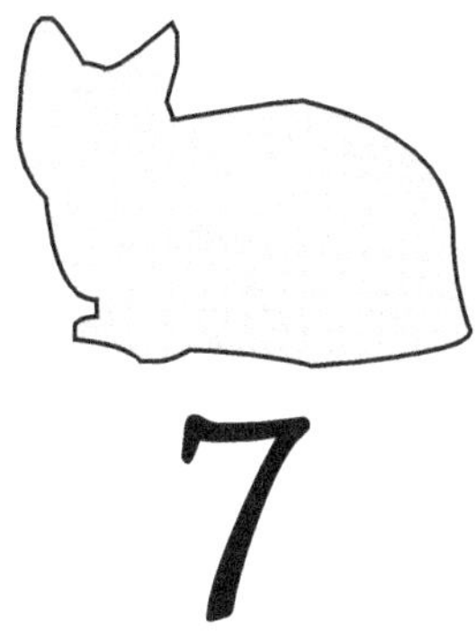

# 7

# It's a Jungle Out There

In God's Country (North Dakota) you can find lots of farm animals, of course, like cows and horses and donkeys. Or, running wild in the badlands out west, you periodically will run across their country cousins twice removed, like maverick elks, native American buffaloes, and mooses . . . or is that meese? (Whatever.) And sometimes in our Statehouse at Bismarck, we have to put up with an occasional jackass. Furthermore, every couple of years, we also have to cope with a plague of smaller unsavory critters like ferrets, weasels, skunks, and polecats. But enough about politics.

I want to tell you about the exotic animals I encountered in Florida. And they weren't in the zoo either. These nightmarish creatures roamed wild and free right there in Slick Willie's backyard, and sometimes invaded the screened-in porch where we felines made our domicile.

That first night in Florida, we slept the sleep of an exhausted fugitive from a chain gang. Along about three in the morning, I was awakened by a loud ripping sound. Although it was a moonless night,

I could see plainly because, as you may know, cats have acute night vision. (In fact, everything about a cat is cute . . . but back to my story.) There, on the floor eating our breakfast which Momma had set out for us last night, was a masked burglar. He was bold and impertinent, calmly finishing off all the food in our dishes and then sneaking back out into the night through the hole in the screen which he had ripped. I stayed on guard for the rest of the night, but that Lone Stranger raccoon didn't show his disguised face again.

Next morning, who do you think got the blame for the damaged screen on the miser's back porch? You guessed it. To add insult to injury, we didn't get our well-deserved breakfast because the heartless warden thought we already had dined sufficiently.

Although Gidget and Angel were scared kittycats, I was courageous enough to exit from that prison cell, out through the ripped screen thanks to "Lone" (I started calling him by his first name). The first things I noticed in the backyard were two huge boulders, covered with a green unhealthy-looking growth. I hopped up on top of one, and was startled to hear it demand, "Get off of me!" Oh my! It turned out to be a giant land turtle, and he claimed to be 400 years old. Judging from the depth of the moss that had accumulated on his north side, I believed him. So I leaped over to the other boulder, only to find out it was his twin brother. These grumpy old codgers, I found out later, were named "Rocky" and "Stony."

About that time, a smelly old goat from across the street arrived and interrupted our discussion. We tried to continue carrying on a polite conversation, but that poor excuse for a deformed elk, whom I christened "Butt-in-ski," just would not shut up. Finally, the twin tortoises got fed up and told me and the goat to go away. And so we did.

I wandered on down to the edge of the swamp where I spied a couple of strange rustic logs floating near the shoreline. The weird thing about them was that their eyes seemed to follow me everywhere I went. Come to think of it, even stranger was the fact that logs had eyes! Then a couple of them started slithering up onto the grass where I was standing. Quick as a flash I recognized them as the deadly allegators I had been warned to shun. Did you ever hear the word "skedaddle"? That's what I did . . . I high tailed it back toward the safety of the porch!

But there, blocking the door, stood the tallest big bird I had ever seen. With disdain it turned its back to me and fluffed out its gigantic tail feathers. It was beautiful, I guess, if you enjoy looking at a bird's butt. I politely greeted this monstrosity, and it replied with the most horrible shrill screech ever heard this side of Fargo, North Dakota. It reminded me of a six-toed sloth scraping its toenails across a chalkboard. Yikes!

So, that was my introduction to the menagerie guarding the penal institution where Gidget, Angel, and I were incarcerated as condemned death row inmates. That second night, and for more than 120 days thereafter, the three of us huddled together in Gidget's bed for comfort and safety. But every time I closed my eyes, it was a nightmare. I envisioned a masked raccoon and a stinky goat sitting on one tortoise-rock, with a toothy allegator perched on the other. A diva peacock in full bloom struck a dramatic pose between her adoring fans, singing a Brahms lullaby at the top of her screechy voice. Oh my, indeed!

Angel and I prevailed on Gidget every night to tell us a bedtime story, and she was happy to do so. My favorite, which she retold so many times that I almost knew it by heart, was about the three amigos who traveled south of the Mason-Dixon Line to rescue a fair maiden named Veronica, who had been kidnapped by a wicked bandito named Wild Willie Wanker.

I suspected that most of the tale was either a made-up story or else it was fictional, but Gidget maintained that it was a true adventure which she personally had participated in. It sounded a bit like a cross between "The Three Mouseketeers" and "The Magnificent

Seven," but I enjoyed hearing the saga every time she dusted it off and served it to us. The three heroes of Gidget's story, who kept trying, night after night, (it was a serial epic) to rescue the fair maiden were swashbucklers with exotic names: Zorro, Leonardo, and Lizzy. I played the role of Leo and the other two tossed a coin to see which was which.

Meanwhile, Momma Roni seemed to be enjoying her stay. She walked through the foliage, dodging the vicious crocs, and picking avocados, bananas, coconuts, orchids, and other edibles. She also went to church every Sunday, where they had pews and song books, and even a robed choir . . . very high class. She also liked to shop, and go to the beach (just to wade, not to get her hair wet). And she made friends with some of the neighbors and Willie's family of six children. There were two boys and four girls, which explains why Willie was a widower on the prowl, for a new cook-maid-housekeeper and part-time wife.

But one day our prayers were answered, and Momma Roni told everybody that this arrangement wasn't going to work out. Although it was sad to leave the children, we packed up our belongings and headed north. The upper Midwest was having a hard winter in 2013-2014, so the trip took much longer than going south did. But it was good to head back home.

# 8

# Who Says You Can't Go Home Again?

The last we saw of Slick Willie was him standing at the end of his driveway, giving us a single-digit good-bye wave. He may have been wishing us a good trip under heaven as he pointed a finger toward the sky, but I kind of doubt it. As Momma Roni headed the loaded-to-the-gills Hyundai due north, we three cats all faced that same direction, aimed our cameras due south, and snapped his picture.

I led the trio in singing a new ditty which I had stayed up all night composing to fit perfectly with the tune of that Civil War classic, "When Johnny Comes Marching Home Again."

"When Momma starts driving home again.
    Meow, Meow,
We'll sing her a brand new 'pome' again,
    Meow, Meow,
Leo will howl, and the Angel will scream,
    Gidget will tell us it's all been a dream,
And we'll spit up hair balls,
    When Momma starts driving home."

It wasn't very far up the Florida coast to Parrish, where Momma's friends, Charles and Donna had a farmhouse. They had lived in the same apartment house in Omaha, Nebraska, many years before, and had kept in touch. Charles was a builder and a farmer, whose main business was haying. I'm not sure what that is, but obviously it has something to do with hay, which is a staple food supply for non-carnivore animals. Personally, I never tried it, but Gidget told me it tastes awful. They had a room in their house just reserved for our family . . . inside! Yes!

Momma and Donna went shopping together and talked a blue streak about the Bible and other deep subjects, most of which went in one of my ears and out the other. I had another interest. Charles and Donna had a stunning feline with long blonde hair, which she liked for her daddy to brush hours on end. She was my first love, and I fell head-over-heels hard for her. Her name was Mokey, and she was so hot-looking that I tagged her "Smokey Mokey." We spent hours romping around in the heather together. She liked me a whole lot too, I think, because she called me "Mr. Fuzzy Pants." From anybody else, that would have been an insult, but from Mokey, it was a term of endearment.

I told her about the extreme dangers which we had survived for four months at the Plantation, highlighting my heroic exploits with the savage allegators, the vicious racoons, and especially the deadly peacock. She regaled me with a hair-raising tale about the native southern coyotes, which she pronounced in three syllables: "ky-oat-teez". We more sophisticated northerners say the name of those skinny canines correctly in two syllables, "ky-oats."

But after three weeks of Momma and Donna checking the weather conditions in the upper portion of the USA to see how high the snow drifts had piled, finally winter started fading and spring arrived, so we had to bid farewell to those good friends. I pledged my undying love to Smokey Mokey and we rode off into the sunset headed for our North Dakota homestead. Often my mind goes back to those 21 happy days, and I wonder how Mokey is getting along, and if she still remembers her Mr. Fuzzy Pants. I hope she stayed clear of that killer coyote, and maybe we'll meet again someday. I hope so.

Although Momma Roni had come equipped with an AAA Trip-Kit and an official Boy Scout compass to keep her on course, she preferred to use the Yogi Berra Rules of the Road. So, we left Parrish, Florida and headed in a generally NNW direction, and when she came to a fork in the road, she took it. We meandered across Alabama and into Mississippi. Before we fell off into the Big Muddy River, we turned right and trekked through Tennessee and on up until we got to the Gateway City of St. Louis, Missouri, very near where we eventually settled down.

The trip started getting tiresome, and our voices started fading about at Kansas City, but Momma steadfastly pressed onward, and her vocal trio kept on singing our patriotic song. The last leg of our journey, through Nebraska and South Dakota seemed to fly by, mainly because Lead-foot Momma had really put the pedal to the metal. We zoomed into North Dakota and lowered our flaps for a landing late on one sunny afternoon in May, after a 5-month safari of high adventure in the uncharted wilderness of the great Southeast.

I'd like to tell you that the mayor of Edgeley met us at the city limits with a brass band and a ticker-tape parade, but I don't think you would swallow that slight exaggeration. So, I'll just stick to the facts. A bunch of our friends, who had kept in touch with our ETA by phone were waiting at the farm for us. They had erected a big sign, "WELCOME HOME RONI!" Joe and Kat were there, and they had kept the place up and running all the time we had been away. Of course, La Rae and Myron were there, and so were Gene and Stella, Tracy and Amanda; even the Norton Methodist Church preacher, Dom, with his wife, Linda, showed up to greet us.

Also in the huge welcoming crowd were Rod and Connie. Rod had advised Momma not to sell the farm and move everything permanently to Florida, as Slick Willie had urged. Momma gave Rod a special hug that day when we returned and told him that he had been right, and she was glad she hadn't sold out, or else we wouldn't have had any place to come home to.

Soon everything settled back into normalcy. Momma and Lash LaRue met daily to toast each other. Joe and Kat dropped by at supper time every few days. Momma resumed attending the Methodist church on Sundays and the Bible study on Tuesday nights. She took good care of the three cats who had been on safari with her, plus (and I am not stretching the truth one tiny little bit here), she fed and nursed somewhere around 100 garage cats, Quonset cats, barn cats, and free-range cats who all gathered at Mastel's place for free room and board.

Every night, Gidget was let outside to hunt for a goose or a moose, Angel slept on her favorite easy chair, and I occupied my privileged spot on Momma Roni's bed. She went back to trolling the internet for a pen pal or someone to share a chicken salad sandwich with, and I snuggled down to snooze in the moonlight, dreaming of Smokey Mokey and what might have been.

# 9

# You Can Observe a Lot by Just Watching

I don't know which world-famous philosopher uttered those words . . . I think it was either Sigmund Freud, Groucho Marx, or Yogi Berra. However, my practice of eavesdropping on Momma Roni's private online romances is the impeccable source of the following chapter in this on-going saga of my nine lives. She was so engrossed in culling through the literally hundreds of potential swains who responded to her bio and pix that she didn't notice me sitting in the shadows of her desk reading every word. What follows here is a sanitized version of those email conversations, with the mushiest parts redacted for the protection of the innocent children and sailors who might stumble across this book and read it some rainy afternoon.

Before I go any farther, let me make one thing crystal clear. There is nobody on this green earth whom I love more than Momma Roni . . . she is right up there equal and on a par with Smokey Mokey! And Momma loves me too. She likes to cuddle me in her arms and calls me her "tiny, little baby boy." Of course, I eat that stuff up, but it actually is a trifle embarrassing because I am about the same age as she is in dog-years. Not that I am saying that Momma is a dog, or anything . . . I think I am getting in too deep here, and I need to put my mouth in reverse and back out. No problem . . . she'll probably edit out this whole paragraph anyhow.

It was June 30, 2014, when a guy in Missouri invested his hard-earned dough and signed up on the "Our Time" dating site. He was looking for a long-term relationship with a Christian woman within 25 miles of his hometown near St. Louis, Missouri. He used the alias of "Quirky Rex" when he signed into the meat market. His picture showed a guy with a short white beard wearing a radio headset. All right, I thought! He's either a fighter pilot or a sports announcer! Imagine my disappointment when we discovered that he was merely a Baptist preacher teaching a Bible lesson over a closed-circuit telephone hook-up. That religious profession was slightly better than an insurance salesman, I reckoned . . . maybe.

Momma noticed that his hometown listed was St. Charles, Missouri. She pinged him back to say that her son (David) had once lived there and worked at Boeing. Then she waited for him to reply . . . and she waited . . . and waited. Finally, she sent a message asking if he had gotten her message. I noticed her fidgeting around the kitchen, and I surmised that she feared she had blown her chances with Quirky Rex by being too forward or something.

Much later that same night, the guy came back online and apologized for the delay. He explained delicately: "One of my greyhounds just had a seizure here in the bedroom, with evacuated bowels and emptied bladder. So, I have been cleaning up the mess. I called the vet but can't get in to see him until morning, if he survives. He seems to have come out of it, and is walking around. He scared me and the other grey, Dottie Moon . . . Yes, I did get your message . . . I liked your pix very much. Too bad MO and ND are so far apart. I'd like to know you better. Oh well, God is in control. Blessings!"

Early on, Quirky Rex had clicked the "Our Time" box to Momma's email saying, "You're my favorite." And she had responded immediately saying, "You're mine." She later confided in me that she wasn't merely talking about him being her favorite. She was actually laying claim to him, asserting that Quirky belonged to her. Oddly enough, the fellow from Missouri had used the name of his greyhound on the dating site, and Momma Roni had used my name, "Big Leo" to sign in. Obviously, these two animal lovers were destined to be together, as compatible as cats and dogs. I mean that in the most positive way: lots of canine-feline matches are wildly successful and successfully wild.

Soon Quirky Rex and Big Leo had shared their real names and telephone numbers, and they were in almost constant communication daily after the sun faded into the west. Curt had commented that it was "too bad that she (Roni) was looking only for an impersonal relationship between friendly pen pals." And she had responded, "Not anymore!" I had feared that her boldness could throw a gallon of cold water on the budding romance, but no. Her frankness just seemed to cause the flower of love to burst into bloom almost overnight.

After about a week of hot and heavy emails and telephone exchanges, both Daddy Curt and Momma Roni started to feel that this was the real deal . . . that Providence was at work and that they were meant to be together. Both of them had skirted saying the magic words, but they had skated on thin ice very close to telling each other how they really felt in their hearts. Finally, it was Daddy Curt who screwed up enough courage one morning to send an email to Momma Roni saying, "Here are the three little words you have been longing to hear . . . " Then, after a very long pause, he wrote, "What's for breakfast?"

After that, there was a whole bunch more of "What's for breakfast?" And, "What's for lunch?" And, "What's for supper?" Sometimes they even stayed up way past my bedtime to say, "What's for a midnight snack?" Daddy Curt sang "The Second Time Around," ala Bing Crosby, and Momma Roni sang "I'm in Love with a Wonderful Guy," from South Pacific. Romantical!

They were so anxious to meet in the flesh, so to speak, that Daddy Curt even tried to figure out a way to fly into Edgeley . . . even though he had vowed never to go through the airport hassle again after one particularly frustrating and maddening day during the Covid-19 outbreak. This latest effort to get on a jet plane flamed out quickly. Then they talked about making a drive and meeting half-way between his house and her house, but that didn't seem to fly either.

Finally, Momma Roni, who was by far the more adventuresome of the pair, made the decision that she would drive the 800 miles from Edgeley to St. Charles to stay for a few days. Daddy Curt was a bit skittish about the idea, but, he figured, if they genuinely loved each other and were dead set on getting married, they probably ought to meet first and get acquainted. So, the date was set and Momma Roni started preparing for her trip to Missouri.

I wondered whether this really was a good idea, but Momma is a cock-eyed optimist. Even when things don't work out as hoped and planned, she will shrug and say, "I thought it was a good idea . . . at the time." This time, however, it did indeed turn out to be a very good idea.

# 10

# Momma Meets Mister Marvelous

Have you heard about the North Dakota farmer who went on the 3-week Garlic Diet? . . . He lost 21 friends! Now I admit this anemic attempt at rural humor doesn't have a whole lot to do with my life's story but hang in there. There is a tenuous link that is coming up, so wait for it.

As we closed the last chapter, Daddy Curt and Momma Roni had found each other on "Our Time," and they were chomping at the bit to meet face to face to find out whether they could see eye to eye on their future. From the day Momma left Edgeley to make the 800-mile trip to St. Charles, until the day she returned with my new Daddy in tow, it was exactly 21 days. See, I told you I would make the connection, and there you have it.

I was not an eyewitness to their goings-on because I was miles away during those three weeks, but I have been able to piece together most of the pertinent details from bits and pieces of conversations which I have overheard with my super-power sense of hearing using these adorably cute ears. Furthermore, if and when any awkward gaps have popped up in this factual narrative, I have cleverly filled them in with some dubiously probable guess-timations.

For one thing, Daddy Curt had been asking the good Lord for a sign to confirm that Momma Roni was the right choice for his spouse. About a week before Momma's maiden voyage to St. Charles, Missouri, he spotted on his office desk a duplicate of a plaque which he had given to some friends 20 years before. It was a memorial to a Bible study group called "Men of Iron" and had a German cross on it with one letter on each crossbar spelling out the word IRON. He rearranged the letters, and there, viola, miraculously appeared the name of his predestined bride-to-be: RONI.

When I looked at that plaque after I came to his house in Missouri, however, all I could see was the word RINO . . . a wild animal that roams the jungles of Africa, or a wishy-washy Republican who roams the halls of Congress. Which reminds me of the dyslexic unemployed hobo who held up a sign reading, "WILL FORK FOR WOOD." Not that I am dissing Daddy or anybody else with vision problems . . . just saying.

When Momma pulled into Daddy's garage on July 24th, she saw a chubby bearded guy wearing a red flannel shirt, sweatpants, and crocs. After her 800-mile non-stop journey, she did not look a whole lot sexier. He led her right into the kitchen, and under the mistletoe-festooned chandelier he hugged her and pledged his troth. As an ordained Baptist preacher, and wanting to keep everything legal and proper, he performed a quicky marriage ceremony, vocalizing all the speaking parts, including Momma's "I dos." Momma just stood there stunned, petrified, and mute. When he had finished the brief ceremony, she uttered her first romantic words into his anxiously awaiting ear, "I need to go to the bathroom." It had been 13 long hours, and, as I mentioned, no potty stops.

Then they walked hand-in-hand into the living room, sat down on the love seat, kicked off their shoes, and put their feet up on the coffee table. Usually this is forbidden behavior, but as this was a special occasion, it went uncorrected. They both had to snicker at the weird sight . . . one pair of bare feet was size 7, and the other pair was size 11. Daddy's was the single-digit foot size, but it's just hereditary because he has smaller bones. Momma comes from up north, which is Big Foot territory, so folks can walk to the barn without bothering with snowshoes.

The next week flew by, with Daddy Curt taking Momma Roni over to his office at the seminary and to the church on Sunday to show her off like a proud tomcat putting on display his litter of newborn kittens. Now, I must pause here to comment on Daddy's financial condition. He was practically bankrupt, following a couple of expensive medical years before his wife, RuthAnn, passed away in 2013. So, unlike Slick Willie the rich millionaire in Florida, Daddy could offer Momma only the one thing that money can't buy . . . POVERTY. As he so elegantly puts it, he was "like the poor snake that didn't have a pit to hiss in!"

In fact, when they went around the corner from the seminary to a neighborhood jewelry store, Daddy had to borrow money from Momma to make a down-payment on an engagement ring. Later, he repaid that loan I understand, and it took him only seven years of belt-tightening.

On August 5th, less than two weeks after they met in person and compared toes, Daddy popped the question. In a man-to-man conversation he had with me later, he spilled the beans about that fateful night. With the engagement ring in his pocket, he took Momma out for a romantic dinner at Applebee's. There he took a photograph of her on his cellphone . . . a prized picture he keeps before him on the desk near his computer. After touring around seeing all the sights of St. Charles and looking for a memorable place to propose, he finally gave it up and drove back to the house on Briargate Drive.

There on the sunporch, overlooking the fenced-in back yard where the greyhounds romped, Daddy got down on one knee and offered Momma his hand in marriage. Or did he ask for her hand in marriage? I can't recall. He did confide in me that he had been afraid that she would say "No," and afraid that she would say "Yes." Not to keep you in suspense too long, Momma Roni paused to think it over for a millisecond, then said, "It seems like a good idea to me." Then she took his hand, helped him get back up onto his feet, and he slipped the ring on her finger. I could tell you that they sealed the deal with a 79-year-old passionate kiss, but I wasn't there, and Daddy didn't tell me that part.

After a couple of weeks of pre-marital bliss, Momma drove over to Kansas City to visit her son, David, and his wife, Denise, and her granddaughters, Gabi and Cali. Momma showed them her new engagement ring, but they weren't overly impressed. I think that they might have been skeptical of Momma's new fiancé, figuring that it wouldn't work out because it was merely a case of being on the rebound, or what you might call "a ricochet romance." She stayed there six days, keeping in touch regularly by phone with her love-sick intended husband, who had deteriorated overnight into a pathetic sad-sack of a human being, if ever there was one.

A couple of days later, after Momma had returned to the arms of her pitiful lover-boy, they packed to make the trip up to Edgeley. On the night before they were to leave early the next morning, Daddy Curt had a severe diabetic episode, wandering around in his skivvies and in a daze while Momma tried to get some sweets into him to overcome his low blood-sugar problem. Frankly, I think that his main difficulty was the daunting thought of driving 800 miles and having to take a potty break every 15 minutes. Momma's solution to that problem - giving him a mason jar and a towel - wasn't a very comforting idea either.

As it turns out, they made the trip without any kind of an incident or accident, and the next chapter will reveal in vivid technicolor the details of the reception that Momma received when she returned to

North Dakota with her bedraggled Baptist preacher-man. So, stay tuned!

*Footnote: Please do not blame me for the "toot-your-own-horn" naming of this preceding chapter. That title was totally Daddy Curt's idea, and I only included it at his insistence.*

*- Leonardo De Cattio*

# 11

# Audition for a Show-Me State Suitor

When word filtered down to the residents of our ranch in North Dakota that Momma Roni was coming back home bringing a new guy to take over as foreman, Gidget called the war cabinet together for a pow-wow. She gaveled the secret meeting to order and checked the attendance roll. Everybody was present and accounted for in alphabetical order: Angel and Gidget and Leo. The two topics on the agenda were: (1) Who the heck is this Missouri turkey whom Momma is bringing here? (2) How the heck can we get rid of him quickly, quietly, and without too much unnecessary bloodshed and/or collateral damage?

As a background to our strategic planning, we reviewed the predecessors in this lead position. Daddy Charlie had been a friendly, popular fellow, who could do almost anything with his hands. And the stuff he didn't know how to do, he read the manual and instructions until he was able to master the task. He was a tireless worker, and in short, good old Daddy Charlie was a "Man's Man." We assigned him the grade of A-plus.

On the other side of the ledger, there was Slick Willie, a tall, handsome, elderly white-haired Southerner originally from the Peach State, with a line of baloney as long as a piece of rope. He could charm the feathers off a bald eagle, and he almost talked his way right into Momma Roni's heart. She barely escaped his clutches in Florida, as I told you about in Chapter 6. We trio of feline vigilantes categorized him as a "Manipulator," and gave him the grade of F-minus.

*Spoiler Alert: By a vote of 2 to 1, we eventually ended up giving the new candidate, Daddy Curt (the self-proclaimed "Mister Marvelous"), the mediocre grade of C-minus, with the succinct admonition: "Needs improvement." But now let me tell you about those ten days he spent with the gang there in Edgeley, North Dakota.*

You only get one chance to make a first impression, I've heard, and the initial impression we got that late afternoon in August was not a good one. When Momma pulled her car into the driveway, the passenger door burst open and a chubby guy carrying a Mason jar and a towel in one hand and a satchel full of OTC meds, prescription drugs, and insulin syringes in the other hand, made a beeline to the facilities. Momma soon followed him carrying the suitcases. In a few minutes, he remembered to get some manners, trekked back out to the car, and lugged in the rest of the luggage. How thoughtful!

Then Momma lined us up for a formal introduction to this guy she called Doctor Curt. I asked and found out that he was not a real MD, or dentist, or even a veterinarian. He claimed to be some other kind of doctor, which apparently didn't help anybody nor make him a lot of money. Angel seemed to warm up to him right away because she is a sucker for flattery and Dr. Curt fawned over her and her purple eyes. I did the gentlemanly thing and batted his outstretched paw.

Gidget deliberately turned her back and displayed total disdain for our uninvited guest.

Tuesday night, Momma took him to "The Harbor" Bible study meeting in Edgeley, where he taught a lesson on Jesus being baptized by John the Baptist. Momma reported to us that he did a great job and that all the attendees were complementary of his sermonizing. However, it seemed to me to be nepotism. Can you believe a Baptist minister would preach his first sermon on John the Baptist? Okay . . . maybe I'm being too picky here, but it just seemed obviously out of line to me.

Everything settled into a routine, until Thursday when Momma Roni and Dr. Curt went into Jamestown to shop at Wal-Mart. While they were there, our year-long drought was finally broken, and the good Lord dumped 3.88 inches of rain on the parched Great Plains of ND in one water-soaked hour. Some folks looked around for a mystical source of this miraculous event, and somebody came up with the bright idea that it was Dr. Curt's prayers that did it, and that he was a genuine, dyed-in-the-wool Rainmaker. In spite of all the buzz and puffy publicity, he never actually made that claim publicly. But he never denied it either.

On the next Sunday, Dr. Curt preached at the Nortonville Methodist Church at 9 o'clock, then drove into Edgeley to preach at 11 o'clock in the Living Word Church. Momma said that he preached the same sermon at both places because, I guess, it was the only one that he had dragged out of the cracker barrel and dusted off to bring with him. It is said that some of the sisters in the church bawled like a baby during his hour-long ovation, and I can believe it. Siting still on those hard wooden benches for 60 minutes would be sheer agony to me and I probably would have shed a tear or two as well.

After ten days our purgatory came to an end; Dr. Curt packed up his meds and Bible and bade us all adieu. Apparently, he had made a big hit with Momma's friends and neighbors, but I can't think why that would be so. Although . . . this indeed is the back-woods territory where folks think that Swedish knock-knock jokes are hilarious, and where grown men choose polka instead of poker. These are the patriotic citizens who think that "Roll Out the Barrel" is our National Anthem, and that Lawrence Welk is a hep cat. So, I guess their taste is just a little bit different . . . or a whole lot different . . . from mine.

Our feline trio was quite disappointed when we heard that Momma was going to drive Dr. Curt back to his home in St. Charles, Missouri. We had tuned up our fiddles and gargled hard cider, and we were all prepared to take him down to the bus station and bid him a fond farewell. I can almost see that heart-rending picture now . . . Dr. Curt is waving goodbye through the back window of the bus while Gidget, Angel and I are 3-part harmonizing on that beautiful old hymn of the church, "Thank God and Greyhound, He's Gone."

# 12

# Trading 2 Dogs for 3 Cats

It was ten days between the time that Momma left to take Daddy Curt back to his house in Missouri until the red-letter day when she returned to launch the North Dakota tornado. Speaking of whirlwinds, near our hometown of Edgeley, the US government has erected an "electricity-producing clean energy wind farm," I think they call it . . . in Washington D.C. gobbledygook language, it's EPCEWF (pronounced "App-shoof"). Whatever. What I'm trying to say is that we started packing the cargo for shipping down to Missouri everything we owned or had borrowed but forgot to return to the rightful owners. (Isn't it weird that you can ship stuff by car, but cargo always goes by ship? That's just one of life's mysteries, I suppose.)

Momma Roni shop-lifted every empty box she could find behind the Piggly-Wiggly store. She would have asked for permission, but time was of the essence, so she cut right through all the red tape and just helped herself. I lost track of all the times she tossed Angel or Gidget or me into an empty veggie carton and started taping it shut before we could holler "Let me out!"

Meanwhile, down in St. Charles, Daddy Curt was getting his house spruced up for a passel of new occupants. He had a company come to clean the carpets . . . especially in the place where Rex had spilled the beans, so to speak. And he dusted off the paper plates and plastic spoons in preparation for his honored guests. He even put a new air freshener in the guest bathroom, so I'm told, although that room is strictly off-limits for family members, so I can't say for sure. The feline rest room is conveniently located on the lower level in the warm furnace room. There are four litter boxes for three cats . . . no awkward waiting with crossed legs for your turn!

Daddy Curt told me that he had burned his britches (or is that bridges?) with all former possible candidates for the office of wife, and he became a guy who was really committed . . . or should be. Momma also was in a tizzy, so maybe they could get adjoining rubber rooms in the funny farm? Having mattresses on the walls seems kind of cozy to me.

When they first talked it over, Momma Roni and Daddy Curt had hoped that their canine and feline friends could live together in the same house, kind of a peaceful co-existence. But upon further research, they discovered that the greyhounds which Daddy had fostered were trained to respond to a bell and race at 45 mph after any moving target . . . like a mechanical rabbit. Apparently, those pooches weren't sophisticated enough to recognize the difference between a fake bunny and a live kitty. So, if the girls (Gidget and Angel) and I had moved into the Briargate Estate, we would have been running for our lives every time the doorbell rang. That would not have ended well nor been a pretty sight. There is just no telling what mortal damage Gidget would have inflicted upon those poor skinny greyhounds. I shudder to think.

Daddy Curt told me that the Scarborough family had started rescuing retired greyhounds years ago when his first wife, RuthAnn, was still alive. Their first pooch was a fawn-colored girl named "Lady

Long Legs," who had raced on the tracks in Florida. When Legs passed away, they adopted a female white racer with black spots, and they renamed her "Dottie Moon. Soon thereafter, they fostered a companion for her, a large brindle guy named, "Quirky Rex" . . . the alias name Daddy had borrowed when he signed up on the Our Time dating site.

It was a somber day in late October 2014, when Daddy called the Rescued Racers people and asked them to come and take Dottie and Rex back to their former kennel-homes in St. Louis County. Daddy had bandaged up Rex's sore hind leg which he had skinned on the back stairs, and he had packed up their bowls and leashes to give to the lady who came to pick them up. He tried to keep a happy face when he waved good-bye, he said, but I know that later on he cried a bit because he missed them. And now, for a few days, his big old house was totally empty, as was his heart except . . .

Except, several times every day, Momma Roni called to cheer him up because she knew he was heartbroken about what circumstances had pushed him into doing. She told him some North Dakota jokes, using her very authentic Swedish accent, and she even sang a love song or two to lighten his melancholy mood.

She took the three of us (Gidget, Angel, and me) aside one evening, and told us that we were moving away from the North Dakota farm for good and always, and that we should be sure to say a nice good-bye to all our good friends, like LaRae and Kat and Joe. She said that we probably would get to see them from time to time, as they might come for a short visit in the summer or maybe around Christmas.

Later that night, Momma Roni spoke confidentially to me when we were alone in her bed. She reminded me of the time when Daddy Charlie had died, and Gidget and Angel had appointed me as the official Comfort Cat. She told me that I had done a very superior job of cheering her up on that occasion, and that now when we got to St. Charles, it was my assignment to be a Comfort Cat to Daddy

Curt, whose heart was sad because he missed Rex and Dottie . . . just as we had missed Charlie and Seara. I promised to do my best, but I couldn't make any promises because I was pretty sure he was a dog-man, not a cat-man. She just smiled and patted my head, and said, "I know that if anyone can do it, you can." It turns out, she was right about that, as she usually is.

I'm not sure whether I should tell you about this or not, but here goes. When we packed up to bring everything of value with us from North Dakota to Missouri, that included Daddy Charlie. Momma Roni had his ashes in a small black box, and she had kept him on a special shelf there at the ranch. When we got ready to leave, she carefully placed him in the car with us in the back seat, where he could ride comfortably. And on Friday, October 26, we pulled into the driveway of 4617 Briargate Drive in St. Charles, Missouri, our new forever home.

I had only one major concern as we arrived. I wondered if Daddy Curt and Daddy Charlie could get along living under the same roof. Well, not living under the same roof . . . I mean dwelling.

# 13

## A 30-day Period of Adjustment

Between Momma and the cats and the furniture arriving in St. Charles on October 26th and the two septuagenarians walking down the church aisle on November 22nd was only one month. Okay, for the sake of you readers who are nitpickers, it wasn't exactly 30 days, but haven't you ever heard of poetic license? Not that this is actually poetry. How about allowing for a "fudge factor?" Daddy Curt has always been a regular customer at the fudge factor factory, and he has manufactured quite a pile of fudge in his day, even in spite of his diabetic condition.

A couple of major face-lifts on the Roni-Curt merger need to be explained in gruesome and agonizing detail . . . and I'm just the gifted author to be able to do justice to this on-going saga.

One problem, which should already have become obvious to you, is their socio-economic conditions which were poles apart. Although she was not exceedingly affluent, Momma Roni was comfortably fixed financially after selling her herd of black angus cattle and auctioning off all that expensive farm equipment. She also knew how to squeeze a dollar until the eagle screamed, and how to economize to the nth degree . . . even to calculating (so it has been rumored) the number of sheets of toilet paper needed in the average week, not counting the uptick during the flu season.

On the other hand, Daddy Curt was kind of laissez-faire when it came to handling money. He just handed his paycheck over to RuthAnn when she was alive, and she unbalanced the books. And when she died, their son Keith was saddled with the thankless chore of paying the bills and trying to make ends meet. It was not easy to do because medical expenses had eaten them alive and somehow their credit cards had gotten pretty much maxed-out.

To complicate the situation, Daddy Curt had the old-fashioned idea that the man of the house should be the sole supporter of the family, and he felt terribly uncomfortable with the fact that Momma was able to put a whole lot more bread in the pot than he could. And in spite of Momma's sincere humility and generosity of spirit, Daddy was adamant that he wanted to keep their bank accounts separate. He acknowledged the need, in fact the imperativeness, of pooling their resources to get the household out of the money pit, but he steadfastly held to the position that her contribution to solvency was merely a temporary loan on an emergency basis. He didn't go so far as to demand a formal agreement signed by a notary public, but his resolve was ironclad - that he did not want to be the junior partner in this historic merger of the houses of Mastel and Scarborough.

Then entered the scene the calm and reasonable voice of their marriage counselor, Pastor Michael. He was a close personal friend of Daddy, and Mike had earned his doctoral degree under Daddy's tutoring at the Pillsbury Seminary, where he was president. Michael listened to the couple's problems, and then, after an hour of Scripture-searching and heart-felt praying, Pastor Mike gave them some spiritual advice that changed Daddy's attitude and saved the future of their marriage. After Pastor Mike left, Daddy and Momma prayed awhile, and vowed to turn the whole situation to the Lord. It must have worked . . . but confidentially, Daddy kept notes in his journal, and after quite a long period of time he was able to justify taking the hand-out from Momma because . . . by his calculations . . . he had repaid his initial loan from her with interest by purchasing the tons of extra groceries needed to feed three hungry cats.

The other problem Momma and Daddy had to deal with was their children's attitude toward two 79-year-old senior citizens falling in love and wanting to get hitched. Love, abstractly, is a wonderful thing of beauty and a joy forever, but hanky-panky between two clunky oldsters can only be classified as ludicrous. *(Parenthetical, Daddy Curt confided in me that hanky-panky did not occur before their marriage on November 22nd. He said there was absolutely no hanky, and very little panky. Besides, he said, don't forget that he had presided over their nuptial vows while standing in the kitchen away back in July, so technically, they were not "living in sin.")*

Daddy's son, Keith, seemed okay with the idea of his father getting remarried only 14 months after his wife had died. His daughter, Karol, also went along with it, although I think somewhat reluctantly and with a bit of skepticism. Both of them agreed to attend the wedding, and, in fact, Keith was Daddy's best man. I'll tell you more about that in the next chapter.

On the first of November, Momma drove Daddy to Kansas City, Kansas, to meet her only child, David. He and his wife Denise, along with their two daughters, Gabi and Cali, were staying temporarily in an apartment while construction on their new home was being completed. It was pretty obvious, so Daddy confided in me, that David was not really enthusiastic about his mother's getting married to an old codger. In fact, David asked Daddy point-blank whether he knew about Bill and his almost getting married to Momma earlier in the year.

Daddy said that he didn't really blame David for questioning their whirlwind romance, because he was genuinely concerned about his mother's well-being. He probably just wanted to protect her from making another boo-boo by getting hitched up to some fortune seeker from Missouri. Daddy Curt put an end to the discussion by saying that he knew all about Slick Willie, because Momma had revealed to him the details of that unfortunate Bill incident. Then Daddy clinched the argument and put a period on the conversation by asserting that he was sure that marriage between him and Momma was the right thing, and that they both were totally confident they were following the will of Almighty God in this matter.

Momma and Daddy returned to our house in a couple of days and continued sorting through the debris. It was so crowded with furniture and boxes that I could barely find a pathway to get from my bed to the litter box without a roadmap. Did I mention that when Momma's truckload of household goods arrived, the house already was crammed to the outer limits? There was lots of stuff from RuthAnn's parents, with more big items overflowing from Keith and Karol's houses (including a grand piano), plus gobs of other miscellaneous junk everywhere you stepped. Then, Momma's treasure trove and furniture from the ranch house showed up, and things got very cozy indeed . . . and very crazy. Speaking of cozy and crazy, the next chapter will tell you all about the wedding ceremony and the ensuing reception. Oh my!

# 14

# For Whom the Wedding Bell Tolls

I will not insult your slightly above room temperature I. Q. by trying to palm off on you that old chestnut about the guy who went to get a marriage license but ended up with a dog license by mistake. That joke is even too corny for Daddy Curt, and besides, I can't think of how the funny punchline goes.

So, I'll just stick to the naked truth and/or the bare facts about the situation. Momma Roni and Daddy Curt's trip to the County Courthouse to get a valid marriage license on November 15th was mostly uneventful. Unfortunately, however, Daddy was shocked (shocked, I tell you!) when it came time to pay the license fee because he had "accidentally" left his billfold in his other pants. Momma had to dip into her mad-money purse to pay the two bucks and get her parking ticket validated. Do you see a repeating pattern starting to develop here?

Frantic preparations for the wedding started swarming all around the proposed bride and groom. Momma enlisted two friends from the Baptist church to plan the shindig . . . Judy and Paula. Daddy and

Momma each prepared a guest list of eyewitnesses to come and view the remains. They made the invitations RSVP, which means, I think, that folks are supposed to dream up some logical fairytale explaining why that won't be able to show up at the festivities.

Momma invited the entire citizenry of Edgeley, North Dakota (pop. 585) and Daddy dug up a handful of his old cronies . . . most of whom would need to be dug up because they already had heeded the call of the golden bells of heaven in lieu of the wedding bells of St. Charles. A couple of decrepit wheelchair-bound oldsters begged off: one because the church didn't have any wheelchair accessibility ramps, and the other guy because he was hopping-mad at his nurse who, he griped, always talked behind his back and pushed him around.

The ceremony was set for Saturday night, November 22, 2014, with Rev. Dr. Michael officiating. Momma's friend from Edgeley, Katrina, was the matron-of-honor. Roni's son, David, brought his daughters, Gabi and Cali, who were flower girls. Daddy's son, Keith, was the best man, but I was his first choice. I reluctantly had to decline that role, however, for two good reasons.

First, we couldn't find a tuxedo in my size. Although my usual handsome long-hair ginger fur coat is okay for everyday wear, I really needed a suit with pockets to carry the wedding rings in. The second reason that I backed out was because it is customary and traditional for the best man to propose a champaign toast to the new bride and groom. (Although, since this was in a Baptist church, no alcoholic beverages would be served . . . just 7-up spiked with Gatorade.) As a bonified rum-lapper myself, I do not know any toasts except the one I learned from the notorious pirate, Blackbeard: "Yo! Ho! Ho! Fifteen men on a dead man's chest." This sea-chanty portrays either an out-of-control scrum in a Rugby match or else the detailed instructions for an elaborate tattoo. Either way, it is totally inappropriate for a formal wedding.

I have in my possession a videotaped recording in technicolor of the wedding ceremony, because Daddy borrowed a bodycam from the police department, and he wore it on his lapel right next to his boot-in-ear. I really do wish that he hadn't turned it on until after he went to the rest room before the ceremony started! . . . Oh well, no big thing.

One weird anamoly about this ceremony occurred at the beginning, when the bride gets walked down the aisle by her father (if he's alive, otherwise he probably wouldn't be available). Or sometimes a close relative or good friend escorts her toward her pending doom. But that night in November, Daddy Curt was the guy walking Momma up the aisle and when the pastor said, "Who giveth this woman to be married to this man?" Daddy answered, "I doeth." Which was his one and only spoken line, and he repeated it several times thereafter.

Then Daddy took the groom's proper position next to the bride, and they answered the pop quiz from the preacher with the correct affirmative answers. Momma kept interrupting the preacher to ask, "Can I kiss him now?" to which the minister shook his head "No." About halfway through the ceremony, Daddy took Momma over to a little table where he presided over a private communion service, sharing crackers and non-alcoholic grape juice . . . remember this is in a Baptist church. Then they came back over in front of Pastor Michael, slipped rings on each other's fingers, and got pronounced husband and wife in the sight of God and those assembled witnesses. "Now," said the pastor, and finally Momma hit Daddy with a big sloppy kiss which "consumed" their marriage . . . I think that's the right term.

Arm in arm, they marched back down the aisle, and everybody followed them downstairs to the Fellowship Hall, which had been set up for 500 or more people. Only about a tenth of that many actually showed up at the hootnanny, but "a good time was had by all," as it was duly reported in the Edgeley newspaper in the next weekly edition.

Most of the wedding party, joined by a couple of other good friends from North Dakota, Gene and Stella, trekked back from the church to the Scarborough mansion to rest up and eat pizza. The bride and groom did not leave immediately for their honeymoon in the Ozarks because they were too pooped. (More about that in the next chapter.) I have videotaped evidence of all the shenanigans which occurred that evening, but I'll spare you those details. Suffice it to state that I have in my possession, safely under lock and key, a huge passel of valuable materials ready to be auctioned off, because Daddy Curt came into the bedroom and just threw his coat over the back of the chair. The police department bodycam was still turned on and running.

How much am I bid?

# 15

# Honeymoon at the Lake of the Ozarks

Have you ever wondered about what the word "honeymoon" means and/or where did it originate? Me too. So I Barney Googled it, and discovered that honeymoon is a compound word . . . kind of like a compound fracture, except without the bone sticking out through the skin. It really is quite simple to figure out, if you just take the time to research its entomology.

"Honey," although it is often used as an expression of affection, really is just a gooey excretion produced by a bee, or some other 6-legged creature. After many years of careful observation, research scientists are still at odds as to which end of the insect is the source of the extracted juice of the pollinated flower. Some claim honey merely is northern bee spit, while others argue that the runny liquid comes from the south end. Either way, does this sound appetizing to you?

"Moon," which shines mostly at night in the western hemisphere, is the dead satellite orbiting the earth every 24 hours or so. It has no light of its own, so it usually remains in the shadow of a greater, more prominent luminary called the sun. The sun, as you probably are aware of, has the first day of the week named after it. The moon lags in second place weekly, and even its name got short-changed from "moon" to "mon."

"Moon" also, according to Webster, is "behaving in a listless or aimless manner." A secondary definition states: "exposure of one's buttocks to another person to insult or amuse."

With these facts held tightly in our sweaty hands, let us now proceed to start to commence to begin to discover a working definition of what a "honeymoon" really is.

A honeymoon is a holiday taken by a newlywed couple which, in many cases, reminds one of gooey insect spit . . . pretty sweet, if you don't stop to think too much about it. Further, a honeymoon reveals that one partner is a bright shining light, and the other guy is a dead dud in the shadows, aimless and listless . . . and occasionally exposing his backside . . . which, frankly is more disgusting than insulting or amusing.

Now let's get on with my story of our old newlyweds, Momma Roni and Daddy Curt. It was cold and threatening to snow when they pulled out of the driveway on Brairgate Drive and headed west toward the Lake of the Ozarks. Daddy had researched exotic and romantic destinations on the internet, and he had booked them into a rather expensive hideaway up on one of the Ozark mountains surrounding the beautiful dragon-shaped lake. They left about mid-morning for the 100-mile journey, so they would have plenty of time and be sure to arrive before dark. Although Momma's Hyundai had some sort of built-in computer guidance system, they also had brought along, just in case, a foldout map Daddy borrowed from AAA.

Ordinarily, I would just keep on telling this story in my own prosaic words, but Daddy has twisted my paw and convinced me that we should insert here the poem he wrote a couple of years ago. So, following is an ode from his book of poultry entitled, "Bard of Briargate."

# Our Honeymoon . . . Whee!

We both were near eighty the day we were wed,
    "Till death do us part" – words the minister said;
I had no idea the end was so soon,
    I barely survived the three-day honeymoon.

So off to the lake in my wife's Hyundai car,
    She drove while I dreamed of the place, not too far;
We'd booked a nice suite with a view – B and B;
    I figured on three nights of sheer ecstasy.

The place we selected was hid in the woods;
    No people around, and no loud neighborhoods;
We got near the place hours before the sun set,
    We were so in love, just like Scarlett and Rhett.

Our G. P. S. Greta knew our destination;
    We planned, when we got there, a big celebration;
But when Greta told us to turn off the road,
    My confidence in her began to erode.

She sent us on gravel, then up a pig path,
    Don't land in the lake . . . though I could use a bath!
"Now Recalculating" our Greta's voice boomed,
    But Roni sped up; and I feared we were doomed!

Yes, this is the right phrase: "All roads were DEAD ends!"
    As Roni zoomed down and around hair-pin bends;
She laughed and cried "Whee!" as she drove in reverse;
    I feared that her Hyundai was really a hearse!

For three hours, or four, we just wandered, quite lost;
    A miracle needed . . . no matter the cost!
Way out in those woods in the hills it was DARK!
    I pled with my wife, "Let's just stop here and park!"

My wife just kept driving while singing with glee,
    Like piggy to market, "Whee, whee, whee, whee, whee!"
Her "wheeing" now echoed my need, which was great;
    I urgently wanted to "rest" . . . urinate.

Then Roni, at last, heard my panicky shout,
    She pulled off the path, and I quickly got out;
"I'll stand here and guide you into a safe place,"
    I said that to her, a fake smile on my face.

Then lo, through the trees, down a lane I could see
    A house with a light on . . . Hooray! Glory be!
I tramped through the jungle and banged on the door;
    My plea, the old man simply chose to ignore.

In front of the guy's house, just out of his sight,
    Stood a rural mail box . . . at just the right height;
I wonder how much the Fed penalty is
    For using a mailbox to take a wet whiz?

At last we contacted the inn on our cell,
    And as is the saying: "All's well that ends well."
Since it was November, the weather was chilly;
    But did we get cold? No: that question is silly!

There Roni beat me in a few games of pool,
    That's how she earned money to pay nursing school;
We drove into town, and we shopped at the mall;
    We found our way back with no problem at all.

I'd marked all the twists and the turns on our route,
    So we could find B and B without a doubt;
I'd colored those mail boxes shiny bright yellow . . .
    It's not what you think! I just sprayed lemon Jello.

On our way back home we drove through a big blizzard;
    But Dakota Roni is a winter wizard!
She brought us home safely without oath or curse;
    The marvelous thing: she drove home in reverse!

Now here are some lessons I learned on our trip:
    My wife drives best backwards; she's quick with a quip;
She hustles at pool; she says "Whee, Whee" to snow . . .
    And mailboxes work if you've just gotta go!

But enough of this fall-de-raw and foolishness! Let us proceed now with my serious memoirs, and I'll tell you about the real climax of Momma Roni and Daddy Curt's honeymoon trip. I was watching out the backdoor when Momma drove up the snow packed, curved driveway. It had been sleeting all day, and the temperature hovered at about zero. In his excitement over arriving home safely, Daddy leaped out of the car and ran up to the door. Then he dropped down onto his knees, and passionately kissed the doorknob.

Have you ever watched the movie, "The Christmas Story," about the kid, Ralphie, who wanted a BB gun, and whose friend, on a double-dog-dare, touched his warm tongue to the frozen steel flagpole? If so, you have a pretty good idea of what happened to Daddy Curt's lips. We had to call 911, and a brave fireman used a pot of hot Chamomile tea to unstick Daddy's mouth from the brass hardware.

They bandaged up his wounds and put his face in a sling, which he proudly wore around the house for a couple of weeks until his birthday on December 10th. That's when he turned 79 and caught up with Momma who had reached that advanced landmark back on April 10th, before we had even heard of Curt Scarborough. When asked about his wounded lips, he would smile slyly and answer, "This is what you get by smooching with Hot-lips Roni!"

Reflecting on this meandering honeymoon tale, I am sort of glad that I've remained a happy and carefree bachelor for these past 14 years. But now, if you'll excuse me for a few minutes, I think I'll curl up and take a short catnap. Maybe I'll be able to rerun those imaginary bliss-filled honeymoon days that I enjoyed with my one and only true love, Smokey Mokey.

Well, a fellow can dream, can't he?

# 16

## Home Improvement Projects

Shakespeare wrote in Julius Caesar, "The evil that men do lives after them, the good is oft interred with their bones." *I put my fascinating narrative on ice momentarily to observe that my secretary, Daddy Curt, is now sitting completely stunned and totally flabbergasted to realize that I am familiar with the Bard of Avon. (With admirable restraint, I resist the urge here to quote that prominent philosopher, Milton Berle, who, when a straight man commented that he was really flabbergasted over Berle's excessive weight, exclaimed, "You gast it, I'm pretty flabber!")*

*For your information, Momma Roni often left the TV on, playing the public service channel, while she busied herself with household chores. I watched between catnaps, which explains how I have been able to soak up lots of culture and other sophisticated trivia from such reliable sources as Masterpiece Theatre and Sesame Street. Hence and ergo, my remarkable minuscule knowledge of the 17th Century classics. Now back to our temporarily suspended story.*

It is my intention here to contrast, with nit-picking accuracy and my usual diplomatic tact, the abilities and aptitudes of Momma's two spouses: Daddy Curt and the late Daddy Charlie. Contrary to the above quote from Bill Shakespeare, it has been my observation that folks tend to make saints out of the dearly departed, rather than to dig up any of their negative attributes. From what I can deduce, Shakespeare missed the mark about good deeds being interred.

In fact, people still speak fondly of Daddy Charlie with appreciation and affection . . . and that's because (for one reason) he was a good guy who could build and fix and repair and rig anything you possibly could throw at him. Daddy Curt, on the other hand, is an all-thumbs klutz as a carpenter, handman, plumber, painter, or anything else which involves manual dexterity and/or physical labor. I've heard it said that preachers get paid money for being good, but Daddy Curt is good for nothing. And I say that sincerely and with genuine love from my whole heart and a tiny part of my liver. I now cite examples to certify the veracity of my unbiased evaluation.

You will remember from earlier that Daddy Curt was financially embarrassed. During the first couple of years of marriage to Momma Roni, everything changed. That first year she rented her farmhouse to preacher Dom and his wife, Linda. Next year, she got a good offer and sold out completely - lock, stock, and barrel. With that cash, she and Daddy were able to pay off his mortgage on 4617 Briargate Drive and liquidate all credit card debts. Then they set about the task of sprucing up the Scarborough house and property.

Outside, they tore down the fence in the backyard where Dottie and Rex had romped. This allowed the herd of deer, which I enjoyed watching out the sunroom window, to graze in our yard, although they apparently preferred to dine in our grouchy neighbor Mike's flower garden. Momma Roni threw corn on the cob out to them, when Mike wasn't looking, but whenever he caught her doing that, he squirted them with a hose. I think he would have liked to squirt Momma, but she gave him the evil-eye, and he wisely restrained himself.

They had a company come to trim off a huge limb that hung over the sunporch, which Momma was sure would crash into us when it got windy. They also gave sick trees a covid shot and raised the canopy of the sycamores. *I always thought a canopy had something to do with a 4-poster bed, but what does an indoor cat know about the outdoors?* Several dead or dying trees got themselves chopped down and put through a woodchipper, which I might add, greatly irritated their occupants, Merle and Pearl, the squirrels. We also had the backyard re-sodded, where the greyhounds had worn off the grass during their daily races. New sod requires watering twice a day, and so Daddy was saddled with the task of lugging the hose around and setting up the spray patterns, while Momma, on his signal, turned the water on and off.

Then they refocused their attention to the inside of the house, which consisted of a 40 by 65-foot structure on two levels. Momma was the engineer-architect of the make-over, and Daddy assisted in a supervisory capacity. Whenever Momma made a suggestion of what they needed to do, Daddy cogitated a bit before concurring, "It seems like a good idea, if we can afford it."

They started by making the sunroom the main hub of the house. Heretofore, it had been the lounge room for the greyhounds, but Momma wanted to make the place like her favorite room back on the homestead in North Dakota. So, they put in new carpets, pained the walls and brought in a dozen plants and vines and shrubs, plus the big oak round table which had occupied the place of honor in Edgeley, with Momma perched in a chair behind it in the corner.

Then they put classy hardwood floors all through the main floor, painted the walls and ceiling, and bought new furniture for the living room. The #2 bedroom became Daddy's office, and the dining room was transformed into a music room. The master bedroom and its bath were up-graded, painted, and carpeted. Everything got changed and rearranged so much that Daddy kept stumbling into stuff during the night as he tried to find out where they had moved the commode. Momma solved that problem in her usual common-sense manner . . . she gifted him a headlamp to attach to his nightcap and a GPS to pin to his nightshirt. Problem solved.

Downstairs, they also put in new carpeting and Momma picked out a huge forest-scene mural to cover the entire west wall of the family room, where they also purchased several new accoutrements designed for sitting down on or lounging on. The downstairs bedroom was transformed into a beautiful guestroom for visitors, and the bathroom was fixed up nicely too. There is a small wet-bar down there, and believe it or not, they even have a place for a "corn-hole" game. Yes, that's what they call it, and no, I haven't got the faintest clue of what that is.

Now please do not get the misconception that I think Daddy Curt is a lazy lout or Freddie the Freeloader. It's just that, whereas Daddy Charlie probably could have done all this work by himself, Daddy Curt has the handicap of being what you might charitably classify as "unskilled labor." For home improvement, I would have highly recommended Daddy Charlie. But for a quick witticism or a stimulating conversation, Daddy Curt would be my first choice. Truthfully, for the kind of a job that Daddy Curt is very good at, he is very good at that kind of a job.

# 17

# Visiting the Veterinarian

Back when I lived in Edgeley, North Dakota, we had a sweetheart of a deal as far as health care was concerned. It wasn't an HMO or an AHC government deal. Have you ever heard of a BVD? That's what we had – Best Veterinary Doctor, and her name was Katrina. Technically, she wasn't actually a licensed medical professional, but she had hung around the Jamestown animal clinic so long that she could explain to you in two short sentences the basic difference between getting yourself spayed and getting neutered. I'll spare you those life-altering details.

Speaking about that subject, Alice once told me about a dumb Bassett hound who eagerly looked forward to visiting the vet because he mistakenly thought his daddy was going to get him tutored. (I pause here to allow time for the inevitable groans at this punny funny by my feline co-conspirator.) She also told me about a veterinarian who specialized in treating snakes for e-reptile dysfunction. Another time, she instructed me on how you can easily identify a dogwood tree . . . by its bark.

*(That material above is a whole lot worse than merely a bunch of bad jokes, it's a cat-astrophe! Therefore, my advice is: just try to ignore her weird sense of humor, and maybe she'll go away.)*

In fact, I think I can come up with better vet jokes than Alice did, with one paw tied behind my arched back. It's easy; I'll just look in a catalog. Or, how about the cat who ate a lemon and turned into a sourpuss? One last shot: Cats are smarter than dogs because dogs cannot operate an MRI machine, but catscan.

Back to ND: Momma's friend, Kat, came out to the ranch fairly often, and on some occasions, she came in a semi-professional capacity. At those times, she would carefully check Gidget, Angel, and me to make sure we were okay, and she would stick us with a needle in our hindquarters. It kind of stung a little bit, but I bravely stifled my meow-ouch because I didn't want Gidget to think I was a sissy. She was army boot leather tough, and took her medicine without a snivel, but Angel whimpered some, until I comforted her by licking her boo-boo.

After Kat had finished the injections or inoculations (if I misspelled that word, just substitute "giving shots") to the indoor cats, she would attempt to round up the estimated 100 feral felines which infested the place. On a good day, she was able to shoot meds into about 50 of the fugitive escapees, but on a bad day . . . only about half that many.

When we moved to St. Charles, Missouri, Momma Roni carefully computer-surfed through all the clinics for cats located within a ten-mile radius of the house. She vetted the vets, rated their ratings, and facilitated their facilities to pick out the best one for her "children". I detested going to the vet because Momma and Daddy would trap me when I was unaware of their nefarious intentions, and they'd stuff me into a small suitcase with a mesh side so I could see out and breathe.

I aways expressed my displeasure by singing "Nobody knows the troubles I've seen," at the top of my lungs all the way to the torture chamber, also known as the vet examination room. Actually, the doctors treated us gently and professionally, but don't mention that in front of my parents. I enjoy sending them on a guilt trip every time they transport me to the vets. After the treatments, I usually sang a different melody on the way back home: something gay like, "Poor Judd Is Dead," or some other show tune.

I will confess that I have been stalling around and kidding about veterinarians because I am putting off one of the saddest incidents in my entire life. I already told you about our losing Daddy Charlie and my friend, Seara back in North Dakota. But losing Angel, whom Daddy Curt called Elizabeth, hurt me even more because she had been my closest confidant and partner-in-crime for several years. She was a few years olde than me, but not quite as old as my other sister, the ninja black tiger cat named Gidget-Alice. In fact, Angel was an equal partner in the courageous trio who survived the Florida fiasco, and she was my faithful, fun playmate every day after we moved to Missouri.

Alice and I and our parents noticed that little Elizabeth was losing weight and throwing up more than her usual hairballs. She just didn't feel up to running and jumping and playing tag with me anymore. Alice told me confidentially that she feared Angel had cancer and had used up all of her nine lives. She advised me to prepare myself for losing our sweet little sister. Daddy and Momma got the cat suitcase out, and we figured they would be taking her to see the vet. I read Elizabeth her favorite poem just before they left. It was Eugene Field's "The Duel" about the gingham dog and the calico cat. She smiled weakly when I got to the part where they ate each other up. I can almost see that smile right now.

I never saw her again after they took her to the vets, but Alice told me that Angel just peacefully drifted off into sleep and the pain of her cancer was over and done. I don't know how Alice knew that. We all cried when Momma and Daddy came home alone, and I tried to comfort everybody, although I guess I probably needed comforting the most. She was my favorite sister, and we usually cuddled up together to sleep when nighttime came. That night I slept by myself, but not very well.

Daddy Curt wrote a poem in his book about the trio of cats from Edgeley, and here is the part about Angel or Elizabeth, as he called her.

# An Angel Named Elizabeth Tailer

Our calico cat with the bright purple eyes;
    A legend of beauty who really liked guys;
She purred and my heart fluttered like a drunk sailor;
    I knew then her name was Elizabeth Tailer.

She was quite an Angel . . . her first given name,
    But teasing poor Leo was her favorite game;
She'd tag him and run away . . . hide by the chair,
    Then leap out like lightning to give him a scare.

She looked so petite, just so tiny and fragile,
    Yet she was quite quick . . . unbelievably agile;
She'd leap, twist, and flip like a brave acrobat;
    I've never seen anyone do it like that!

But one day Elizabeth got very ill,
    We hoped that the vet could just give her a pill;
We cried when we held her and said our good-byes;
    I'll never forget my Elizabeth's eyes.

A final word about Elizabeth. Sometimes when it's really quiet and everyone is asleep, I prowl through the living room and sneak up next to the love seat. I pause a minute to peek around the corner, and just for an instant I think I can see an Angel just getting ready to pounce out and scare the heck out of me. I really miss her . . . that beautiful calico was absolutely purr-fect!

# 18

# Routine, But Not Necessarily Hum-drum

Daddy Curt is kind of obsessively organized (OCD), but Momma Roni is more laid-back and relaxed . . . except when she catches me up on the eating table on the sunporch. This household maintains a pretty rigid routine, which, coincidentally, has in it the tell-tale letters: RUT. I'm not implying that we're in a rut around here . . . I'm saying it flat out! Let me illustrate by sharing a typical week's activities.

Every weekday begins at 7 a.m. with Daddy Curt staggering out of his recliner into the bathroom for a pitstop. He sleeps in that chair because of his sinus condition, arthritis, neuralgia, and the heartbreak of psoriasis. Momma Roni sleeps in the 4-poster, almost like a normal person. Then Daddy goes back to the kitchen and eats a bowl of bran and two pieces of cinnamon toast, washed down with a couple of big cups of strong black coffee which Momma fixed-up for him the previous night before she retired. Then he steps out through the garage to fetch the Post-Dispatch, which is a left-leaning Democrat . . . but it's the only newspaper in town.

He downs his food while listening to the news on KMOX, then turns it off, and reads his Bible passages for the day. Then he prays for the folks on his prayer list, and writes a few lines in his personal journal. During this time, I either sit on the table watching him or I sit in his lap. I do not wish to be rude here, but frankly, there isn't that much room on his lap these days. Just a couple more pounds and he'll be sitting in his own lap.

When he finishes his quiet devotional time, he reads the toilet-paper Post, and loses whatever spiritual progress he had achieved during the preceding thirty minutes. First, he reads the comics, then the sports, and if he has the stomach for it, he scans the editorial page and the local news. By this time, around 8:30, Momma Roni completes her beauty rest and makes an appearance, greeting him a cheery "Good morning!" to which he replies, "What's for breakfast?" Her unwavering response is, "I love you too, darling." I do my best to interrupt this unseemly lollygagging to remind her that it's time for my breakfast. She obliges with some yummy treats, followed by serving my favorite fish-chicken combo from a tin can.

They talk awhile, interrupted by Daddy's visit to the facilities to brush his teeth or whatever, and then they plan out the day's activities. Unless they have a doctor's appointment, Daddy works until noon in his office before taking a shower and getting dressed, and Momma reads the paper and talks on the phone and writes checks. Afternoons are more of the same until they take time out for a nap. They used to call it "Pillow Talk," but now they don't talk much and there's no pillow involved, so it's just plain snoozing.

In the evening, they listen to CD's playing Mancini or Willie Nelson, and they enjoy a romantic supper with candlelight and wine. Then they catch a baseball game, or football, and watch the news. Afterward, Momma takes the cats back to the kitchen and throws the dishes into the sink, promising to wash them tomorrow. Finally, she prepares the coffeepot for the next morning, while Daddy watches Carol Burnett and then puts on his sleep mask and calls it a day.

Weekends are not too much different except on Sunday morning, Daddy "shaves for Jesus," and puts on his go-to-meeting clothes. He watches a long-dead Baptist minister from Memphis preach a recorded sermon from the grave, and then both of them, accompanied by whichever felines they can corral, go into Daddy's office to watch the Sunday worship service from Morning Star Church where their son, Keith, is one of the pastors. Following that family time, Daddy carries out his one and only mandatory and obligatory assigned chore for the family household . . . he winds the grandfather clock in the front foyer.

This routine, although somewhat boring, also is comforting and comfortable, as apparently old people don't like to do anything too stimulating or exciting, which might give them an attack of some kind or throw them into a coma or something. About once a week, Daddy makes a trip to the bank, and then goes for a twelve-mile drive around the immediate neighborhood. If he doesn't drive his old Chrysler at least once a week, the battery dies and he has to call AAA, so he makes this sight-seeing trip religiously. Momma's car doesn't have that problem because she goes to Wal-Mart or Aldi's or the Post Office every couple of days.

The Welcome mat is always out at the Scarborough house, and we do have folks drop in here from time to time. Like the neighbor across the cul-de-sac, Linda, or our friend Judy (who always brings goodies for us), or Patti, who is a schoolteacher and who helps Daddy with his business.

Special guests, who come annually (more or less) include our old ND friends, Kat and Joe, who always bring along their friendly dog, Jenna. She and I are not what you would call close friends, but we do tolerate each other for the few days while she is an interloper on my territory.

Daddy's son, Keith, and his wife, Lorilise, drop by occasionally . . . especially on holidays. Momma's son, David and his wife, Denise, and their daughters (Gabi and Cali) drive over from Kansas for a few days around Independence Day and Christmas. They bring along with them other members of their clan including a chihuahua named Pixie, and the last time that tiny dog brought along a miniature pet of her own . . . a teeny-weeny cup-sized canine they named Tinker Bell. I didn't mind too much Pixie's yip-yips, but I was a bit skittish around the midget, (Tinkle is what I called her, for one obvious damp reason) because I was afraid that I might accidentally step on her with my size ten-and-a-half paw and squash her like a stink bug.

One time, when we had a house full of guests, one of them carelessly left the front door open, and I saw my chance to get out of the melee. I sneaked into the backyard, but Momma spotted me from her lookout in the sunporch. Daddy searched the neighborhood, frantically calling my name. Finally, he gave up in despair, only to come back inside to find me innocently snoozing by the fireplace. Truthfully, I did not like it very much outside. The grass tickled my paws.

Yes, we may be in a RUT around this place. But I can't think of a better rut in the entire USA where I'd rather be. But now, if you'll pardon me, I see by the grandfather clock in the foyer that it is exactly and precisely the regular time for my mid-morning snack. Daddy is a stickler about keeping everything on his schedule, and I certainly do not want to be the one in the family who disappoints him or who causes him undue distress. The Lord knows that he already is a nervous wretch.

# 19

## Alice N. Wanderland

Alice N. Wanderland (nee Gidget) was born, she told me, in the Bad Lands of North Dakota on April 24, 2002. She grew up tough and smart and independent. When she arrived on the Mastel Ranch a couple of years later, Daddy Charlie and Momma Roni didn't adopt her . . . she adopted them, and she graciously bestowed upon that entire outfit the benefit of her wisdom and knowledge, and all-around know-how.

When I arrived on the scene in 2010, she already had established her reputation as the ramrod of the animal kingdom in La Moure County and adjoining rangelands. At first, she barely acknowledged that I even existed in her universe, but by and by she warmed up to my irresistible charm and kind of took me under her wing, so to speak. I think she somehow foresaw into the future and recognized that someday I would succeed her perched on the top level of the cat tower.

When Angel-Elizabeth went away, only the two of us remained to tell the next generation the adventures we had in North Dakota and

Florida and other exotic locations. So, Alice began finding more and more time to tutor me about the facts of life and to mentor me on the secrets of how to survive and thrive on the mean streets . . . which actually seemed unnecessary to me, because neither one of us ever got out of the house in St. Charles, except to go to the animal clinic to get our checkup and annual rabies shots.

Alice lived to the ripe old cat-age of 19, which figures out to be 92 in people years. Let me educate you, just in case you missed this lesson in calculus in junior high school. It is easy to translate dog years into people years, because all you have to do is multiply the number of years that the mutt has been around by seven. So, if Fido has lived say ten pooch years, that is the equivalent of 70 human years. Simple!

But if you are trying to figure out cat years, it's not so easy to translate, but here goes. A 1-year-old cat is age15 in people years, and a 2-year-old cat is 24 in people years, which is within just a few months of being eligible to run for the U. S. Congress. And, may I add, most felines I know could probably do a better job than some of the dodos we send off to Washington, D.C. But I got sidetracked there, sorry! It's an election year, and everybody has gone sort of goofy trying to mute out all those political ads on TV.

Continuing the math lesson: After the second cat year, when we reach the age of 24 for humans, you just add on four people years for every cat year. So, in the case of Alice, she turned 24 in 2004, and in the next 17 years, she aged 68 years (17 X 4 = 68, if my ciphering is accurate, and I think it is because Daddy Curt double-checked me on his Chinese abacus.) Correct answer: 24 plus 68 equals 92. Class dismissed.

The last few months of Alice's action-packed life were spent in quiet retirement, during which she tried to stuff into my brain all the wisdom and know-how which she had accumulated in her 92 years of experience. She retold me about her adventures up in North Dakota, including the time when she got caught out in the infamous Great Plains Blizzard with temperatures way below zero. She had burrowed down inside a haystack to keep warm, and she succeeded in doing so . . except for the tips of her ears.

If you ever saw Alice, you could not miss her tippy ears, which sort of bent over in the middle and pointed in the direction where was looking. Some foolish barnyard animals started calling her "Tippy" behind her back, but they kept that comment to themselves because she had put the fear of the Lord into them on previous occasions when they got out of line.

And, of course, at my insistence she often recounted the details of how she won the purple heart by defeating that killer moose, Roscoe . . . and how she ate the whole thing. It was awe-inspiring to hear her description of how she was able to chew-up and choke-down his huge rack of antlers. Totally awesome!

As I mentioned, in the summer of 2021, Alice's swagger and confident take-charge attitude began to fade little by little and day by day. She confided in me that she would not be with us much longer, and that she wanted me to be brave and ready to take over for her when she was gone. I protested for two reasons. Mainly, because I didn't want her to go, and second . . . I was pretty positive that I wasn't up to the task of taking over her responsible position as the wise sagacious voice and the calm reassuring presence that this family at the Scarborough house so desperately needed.

One day in September, she advised me that her time was short, and by now, Momma Roni had noticed the tell-tale signs. She brought Alice's litter box up from the furnace room, so the elderly cat wouldn't have to struggle with the stairs. Momma also made a soft bed on the sunporch and served up Alice's favorite food, but she wouldn't eat. Alice really wanted to go down into the furnace room, way back where it was dark, and fade away without bothering anybody. But Momma shut the doors into the sunroom to keep her up here where we could take care of her and let her know how much we loved her.

One morning, it was September 25, 2021, Daddy Curt came out early to check on Alice, and he found that she had passed away in the night. He told Momma, and we all cried awhile, and then Momma picked up Alice and wrapped her in her favorite blanket. Momma called her friend, C. J. . . . the vacuum cleaner lady . . . who came to take our Alice to her farm in Bourbon, Missouri, where she buried Alice in a beautiful spot with flowers growing over her grave. (Confidentially, this is the pleasant spot which Momma Roni thinks might be a good place for her and Daddy Charlie to be laid to rest someday.)

I miss Alice more than I can write, and I am doing my best to fill her shoes . . . I mean her paws. She was my example, my guru, my hero . . . and during those last few years when we were the last cats from North Dakota transplanted in Missouri . . . she was my very best friend. Daddy Curt misses her too, as you can see from the following poem.

# Black Tiger Cat with Tippy Ears

Black tiger cat with tippy ears,
Her life is full . . . a lot of years!
And yet she runs and jumps and plays,
Then finds the sun to while her days.

I've named her Alice Wanderland;
She's silent, graceful, wise, and grand;
But Gidget was her maiden name,
Before into my home she came.

In North Dakota she was raised,
Where snow is deep, and roads are glazed;
An outdoor cat, she's brave and bold,
Ignoring blizzard, braving cold.

One wintry night she failed to hurry
To find her home so warm and purry;
The weather out was cold and nippy,
Her ears got frosty, numb, and tippy.

Her hunting through the countryside,
Brought admiration far and wide;
She gobbled gophers and a goose;
And once, she said, she ate a moose.

But then, without a judge or jury,
        Her Mom brought Alice to Missouri,
Where she's confined inside a house;
        No gophers, geese; no, not a mouse!

So now she sits upon my lap,
        Or jumps upon my bed to nap;
She climbs up high upon her perch,
        And sleeps as if she was in church.

Unlike our younger cat, who chases
        Balls and toys and twine and laces;
Now Alice sits upon her cushion,
        And lets the humans do the pushin'.

I wonder, as I search her eyes,
        How did she get so smart and wise
It must be that she listened well
        To hear the tales I love to tell.

**Final Good-bye: September 25, 2021**

Today we said "Good-bye" to Alice,
        The reigning queen of Scarborough palace.
We laid her on a comfy quilt,
        And felt our hearts begin to wilt.

She lived with us; enhanced our love;
        We'll see her someday up above;
She blessed our lives for nineteen years,
        Our Alice with the tippy ears.

# 20

# Anastasia Katinova

Two or three days after the passing away of our beloved Alice, Momma Roni and Daddy Curt conferred about my lonely state of being the sole representatives of my clan. They came to the conclusion that we ought to get another feline, which would not be an insult to Alice (nobody could ever take her place), but it would be more of a compliment to her memory. I had mixed feelings about this prospect, but after thinking it over for a while, I warmed up to the idea. Then I got excited, thinking about getting a new baby brother, whom I could take fishing and play ball with, and teach lots of other kittenhood stuff. As a full-blooded Italian ginger cat (which my name, Leonardo De Cattio reveals), I even picked the perfect name for my new brother . . . Filippo Felini. Wow, I thought, this is going to be a blast!

As usual, Momma went to her computer to shop, and she pulled up three or four pet adoption sites. She showed Daddy the best one she could find, which was located not too far away over on Mid-Rivers Mall Drive. On-line, they checked out dozens of candidates, including some very promising gingers and calicos, but Daddy sort of zeroed in on a particular black and white cat whose name was Daisy . . . kind of a weird name for a male cat, I opined. That very afternoon, they drove over to the adoption agency, and the first thing they spotted in the big cage was the very tuxedo which Daddy had fallen for online. The lady in charge of the orphanage brought Daisy over to get acquainted with Momma and Daddy in a private viewing cubicle. After a brief howdy-do session, Momma wanted to look at some other possibilities, but Daddy said, "What for?" His mind was already made up, Daisy was for him.

So, they negotiated a deal with the proprietor and paid only ten dollars to bail Daisy out of jail. The usual fee was fifty dollars, but since Daisy had been there about six months already, and they were tired of feeding her six meals a day, the lady charged them only ten bucks. Momma and Daddy brought Daisy home in a hutch, and they left her in there for several hours so she could get used to me and vice-versa. It was during this get-acquainted interval when I discovered to my great disappointment that Daisy was a girl cat.

I had so much counted on getting a brother, and now . . . another sister. Angel-Elizabeth and Gidget-Alice were fine and dandy, but surely not three in a row! They, along with Momma always had formed a majority and outvoted Daddy and me on every major decision. But for three days, the males had outnumbered Momma two to one . . . until female Daisy arrived on the scene to tie the score, which meant that Daddy and I would lose every election because tied votes always go to the weaker gender, as a matter of Midwestern courtesy.

Instead of christening her with a new Italian name, like mine, our parents named their new tuxedo cat "Anastasia Katinova", obviously a Russian moniker from behind the iron curtain. She was a black cat which, it appeared to me, somebody had picked her up by the tail and the scruff of the neck and dipped her into a pot of white paint. She had a line all around her entire body: black on the top and white on the bottom. Even her face was two-toned, leaving her chin white but with her eyes covered by a black mask like the Lone Ranger.

When they finally paroled her from the carrying cage, she and I had a frank discussion in which I informed her who was in charge around here, since Alice had gone. She told me that she had been a free-range cat running wild for several months before an animal control officer captured her and put her in the hoosegow for adoption. She said that she hadn't fit in very well, and so she had stayed at the warden's house for a time until she got acclimated, which didn't sound like something I would enjoy or look forward to.

It didn't take long for her to get used to the relaxed routine of the Scarborough household. One bad habit that I never could break her of is this: she always would come whenever Daddy called her shortened name, "Annie" (as in Little Orphan). She never did catch on that cats NEVER come when they are called because nobody can tell us what to do or when to do it. She and Daddy liked to play games together, like "Bye-bye Birdie" where she chased a fake bird on a string which he twirled around in the room and when she finally caught it . . . it wasn't edible.

Speaking of eating, she had an overly-hearty appetite, probably due to those lean and hungry years she spent on the street, searching all the time for her next meal. All the food she consumed broke the family's budget, I imagine, and the calories started showing up on her hips and elsewhere. I commenced calling her affectionate nicknames like "Chubbo" and "Blimpo." Sometimes, on those days when she ate my own personal treats, I subtly encouraged her to go on a diet by calling her "Miss Goodyear of 1935" and "Hildegard Hindenburg."

Annie is very skittish around strangers, even to this day, and she's been here in this house since September 28, 2021 . . . which makes her almost five years old. It was fitting somehow, in my opinion, that Annie was born on Groundhog's Day in 2020. Get it? . . . "Ground HOG!" She is a scaredy cat, for sure, especially of C. J. - the very good friend of

Momma and Daddy, who comes every week to clean and change our litter boxes. Although Annie has been here for three years, and C. J. has been in this house a hundred times or more, they never have been introduced formally . . . or even seen each other face to face. As soon as C. J. arrives, Annie high-tails it to her hideaway in the furnace room, and she doesn't come out until the "Vacuum Cleaner Lady," as Annie calls her, leaves the premises.

Let me illustrate. We just got past watching Halloween horror movies with Svengoolie, during which time Annie sat on Daddy's lap (the usual spot where she parks herself every time he sits down.) Annie and I thought it might be a good idea to dress up in a costume and go "trick or treating" back and forth between Momma and Daddy, begging for more yummy treats. We considered being Frankenstein or Dracula or The Ghost of Mr. Chicken. But I decided to be The Creature from the Black Lagoon, which was a bit of a stretch, considering my rather svelte physique and aversion to water. Annie pondered for quite a while, trying to come up with the scariest outfit that she could think of. Finally, she made her decision. She worked all afternoon, then came up out of the basement to go "trick or treating" dressed up as a vacuum cleaner.

Against my better judgment, the following is Daddy's short poem about Annie. He persistently insists on horning in on my personal memoirs with his Robert Frost imitations . . . even though it means more typing with his arthritic shoulder, which he hurt by patting himself on the back.

# Orphan Annie

The cat in our house is the true Anastasia,
    The Duchess from Russia in Southwestern Asia;
Although this seems odd and, in fact, it's uncanny;
    She goes by the alias name "Orphan Annie."

When Alice, at nineteen, departed this life,
    It cut us in heart like a razor-sharp knife;
So we went to a place for adopting a pet,
    And I said: "That's the one which we surely should get!"

I'd seen a nice photo of her on computer,
    And knew in an instant, no cat could be cuter.
We drove to our house, and she knew right away
    That this was her home, and that she's here to stay.

This black and white kitty they call a Tuxedo,
    Zooms all through the house like a navy torpedo;
She skids on the hardwood while chasing a bug,
    Then all of a sudden, she flops on the rug.

She eats all the time and now looks a bit sturdy,
    Her favorite games are "Paw-Paw" and "Bye, Birdie."
She licks Mister Leo, but sometimes picks fights,
    And stalks Momma's toes just to take tiny bites.

She stakes out a claim on her Daddy's big chair,
Then sits on his lap without worry or care;
But when a strange person arrives at the house,
She hides in the basement as still as a mouse.

"But how did you know she's the one," people ask,
"Her white face half-hidden by that velvet mask?"
"Quite simple," I answered, "She said not a word . . .
But captured my heart when sweet Annie first purred."

# 21

## He's All Right Now

At the advanced ages of Daddy Curt and Momma Roni, it's almost inevitable and unavoidable that they'll end up in the emergency room and/or the hospital sooner or later. For instance, one Saturday evening after supper, Daddy started complaining about pain and pressure across his chest. At first, he thought it might be that his shoulder holster was too tight, but that wasn't it, so he took a couple of gas pills. No luck, so finally he agreed, and Momma called 911. A team of firemen showed up at the front door, made him swallow a couple of baby aspirins, and hauled him off in an ambulance to the emergency room at BJC . . . which stands for Big Jewish Clinic, I think, but he didn't mind that even though he is a staunch Baptist.

They kept him overnight and on Monday, the sturgeon implanted a stent into one of his blood vessels by going up through his leg, which was the scenic route. I wondered why they didn't cut directly into his bosom, but what do I know? I'm just a CC (Comfort Cat), not an MD.

Daddy Curt told me that with the peek-a-boo hospital gown he had to wear, it was proper and fitting that the sign outside his door read, "ICU." He said that a man across the hall from his room froze to death during the night because he accidentally kicked off his blanket, and he didn't re-cover. He also told me about his roommate who survived a terrible tractor accident, and they had to amputate his left ear and his left arm, and his left leg. "He's all right now," he giggled, but I failed to see the humor in that remark . . . until about 30 minutes later.

Momma Roni ended up in the hospital three times during the decade she has lived here in Missouri. The first time, she got an excruciating pain in the neck (not Daddy . . . a different pain in the neck). She was agonizing and suffering beyond human endurance, and so Daddy drove her to Protest West Hospital Emergency, and checked her in. She sat moaning in the waiting room for more than two hours, until finally an examination room opened up. In there, she waited another eternity-long 68 minutes until a nurse came in and told her to stick out her tongue, which she was happily in the mood to do. Then the nurse left the room to confer with the physician and came back in half an hour with a couple of aspirins and told her to go back home. If the pain didn't get any better, they said, Momma could come back tomorrow between 3 and 4 a.m., when they weren't so busy.

Daddy told me that he was sitting in a chair in Momma's examination room while she was sitting on the bed with her legs dangling over the side. Suddenly, he was startled out of his wits when she yelled at the top of her North Dakota lungs an extremely long and loud, "POO-POO!" Except she didn't exactly say Poo-poo, but I have used a sanitized synonym here because this book is rated "G" for General Audiences. Daddy (a Baptist preacher in generally good standing with most of the brethren) just sat there motionless as Momma's expletive echoed throughout the entire hospital. He did not move a muscle or show any emotional response . . . pretending that he was just a Good Samaritan who had rescued some poor unfortunate woman beside the road, and out of the goodness of his heart toward a total stranger in need, had transported her to the emergency room free of charge.

Momma also showed how brave and tough she is by having both her knees replaced with some sort of plastic-steel contraption. She told me that, although her previous hip replacement surgery in North Dakota had gone like a breeze, practically painless by comparison, getting her knees altered into bionic joints hurt like the dickens . . . which, I take it, has something to do with the torments of the hot place, also which I am censoring out of this narrative. I am happy to report that Momma always got to feeling better after my personal therapy was applied for a few nights, as I sat on her lap through those long early morning hours and snuggled my head up under her chin. I think she got feeling better because she absorbed my warm love for her, and I know I felt proud knowing that, as the family's official Comfort Cat, once again I had been able to pull someone through a major health crisis into a full recovery . . . without a blanket.

I have a theory about why over seven million American humans are hobbling around on knee replacements, but you hardly ever hear of a cat having that surgical procedure. The reason is simple mathematics. Bi-peds have to use their legs twice as much as those of us with four feet, and, coincidentally, with the same number of legs to match. If you use something twice as much, it only lasts half as long. So, humans should start walking on all fours. Viola! What a great scientific breakthrough! I feel like that world-famous researcher who discovered a cure for which there is no known disease! Maybe I should write a paper and send the idea to the Mayo Clinic where, Daddy tells me, the head doctor there is a beautiful blonde named Virginia.

When Momma came back to the house in St. Charles, MO after both of her knee-replacement operations, she refused to use crutches, instead she insisted on hopping around the house on one foot. For a few days, Denise, her daughter-in-law came to cook and to supervise Momma's exercise regimen. Daddy's job: merely to help her on and off the adult-sized potty chair beside the bed, but I'm forbidden from painting a word picture of that scene, so I'll just move on.

You will have noticed, no doubt, that the preceding two chapters contained Daddy's poems about Alice and Annie. I reluctantly relented and allowed him permission to include his amateurish attempts at versifying on one condition. The stipulation is that we also include as the final chapter in these Memoirs the very first poem which he wrote as he began his poetic career. So, here following you'll be able to enjoy "A Ginger Cat upon My Lap," which, in case you haven't figured it out yet, refers to yours truly. I also have included a copy of the hand-made Father's Day card which Annie and I sent to Daddy Curt last June.

A final word: I am going into the animal hospital in St. Louis County on November 12, 2024 . . . about a week from now, to have a radiation treatment for my hyper-thyroid condition. They tell us I'll have to stay over for a night or two, which I am not looking forward to. However, the vet claims it will fix the problem, and that I'll be 100% cured. If so, and I have faith to believe that it is so, perhaps I'll team up with Daddy again to write my memoirs, part two. At any rate, I expect to be back home by the middle of the month to celebrate Thanksgiving and Christmas with my family. Turkey! . . . my favorite . . . (not Daddy, I'm referring to the meat.) Although?

Meanwhile, it you happen to phone Momma to ask how Leonardo is doing after his ordeal in the hospital, I am sure she'll be happy to report to you, "He's all right now."

# A Ginger Cat Upon My Lap

Each morning at the break of day,
I slip out to my porch to pray;
And there I read and think and nap;
A ginger cat upon my lap.

We watch the sun rise o'er the trees,
Their branches swaying in the breeze;
The sycamore that sheds its bark,
Awakes to shoo away the dark.

Then from a hole, out pops a squirrel,
We've named that little fur-ball Merle,
He may be boy; he may be girl;
Perhaps his name is Minnie Pearl?

My cat and I soon spot a rabbit;
We've given him the name of Abbott;
He's really quite a hoppy fellow;
His lady friend, we call Costello.

Then bye and bye we see a deer,
A queen she is, named Guinevere;
One day she came just after dawn,
To introduce her new-born fawn.

Too soon the neighborhood awakes,
Loud banging sounds the trash-man makes;
The coffee perks; the paper guy,
Squeals tires and honks while passing by.

Then Roni comes – my lovely wife;
The shining star of my great life;
She says, "Good morning" with a smile,
We sit and visit for a while.

Our children and our grandkids too,
Think we are old and bored and blue;
But we are happy and alert;
Just Roni and her man named Curt.

When sunset comes and day is done;
We look upon our lives as fun;
We do whatever things we please;
With ginger cat upon our knees.

# Father's Day Card from Leo and Annie

Some holiday cards are quite
mushy and sappy,
While others are crude and some
really are crappy!
So we wrote our own just to
make our Dad happy;
We're glad on this Father's Day,
you are our pappy!

Leo the Lover

Annie the Flopper

www.ingramcontent.com/pod-product-compliance
Lightning Source LLC
Chambersburg PA
CBHW061747050726
47598CB00002B/614

* 9 7 8 1 6 6 2 9 5 9 5 4 7 *